TRANSFORM YOUR HEALTH BUSINESS

Multiply profits
and **grow your practice**
with less stress and
more freedom

PAUL
BAKER

RETHINK PRESS

First published in Great Britain in 2019 by
Rethink Press (www.rethinkpress.com)

Graphic design by Warren Eades/Illustration by Toucan Design

Praise

'Behind every success there is a process. In this book Paul has identified that process for success. Often, people stumble through the process. What Paul has achieved with this excellent book is to define the steps in a concise, easy-to-follow manner.

When I read this book, I was delighted that someone had translated the essence of our success at Fitness First PLC, into a simple growth model for the health industry.

The five-step Practice with Profit Way, based on therapists' motivations of helping people and connecting through valuable relationships with self-funding patients, is an extremely cost-effective way to grow and scale any health business.

Read this book if you want to build a motivated and high-performing therapy team that achieves your health business growth targets.'

— **Steve Jones**, entrepreneur, international speaker, author of *Turning on Your P.R.O.F.I.T.S. Tap* and *Mapping Motivation for Engagement,* and founder of Skills for Business Training Ltd

'They say that if you get one good idea out of any book it has been worth the effort. This book is packed with sound advice and should be compulsory reading for anyone in business-to-business or consumer-to-consumer sales. The principles outlined here apply not only to physiotherapists, but to opticians, veterinarians and cognitive behavioural therapists – indeed, to any business where there is no tangible product and staff are selling their time. Modern-day knowledge workers (including physiotherapists) want to make a difference. Their purpose is usually more important than the money (as long as the financial returns are at an acceptable level). This book will help employers recognise and tap into this rich seam of motivation and creativity.

Paul, where were you fifty years ago, when I needed you most?'

— **Alan Glover**, entrepreneur, trainer and coach,
The Elenchus Approach

'Whether you're new to private practice or have been in the game for years, this will become your go-to manual.

It's packed full of advice, education and strategies to accelerate your health business and help you build a motivated and high-performing therapy team, showing you how to put your team and patients at the centre of your growth plans and decisions.

I only wish this book had been written when I opened my practice sixteen years ago. There's no better way to learn than from someone who has experienced it first hand and overcome all the obstacles.

Paul is straight-talking and generous with his knowledge and experience. This is a book that's jam-packed full of value, and which you'll definitely read more than once.'

— **Amanda Hatt**, entrepreneur, health business owner and leader, Hatt Clinic

'Before reading Paul's book, the biggest problem I had was motivating the team to consistently achieve our growth targets. Since reading this book and implementing the Practice with Profit Way in our health business, our therapists have become increasingly motivated to meet our growth targets, through higher conversion rates, increased patient visit averages and improved patient retention within the clinic. These, combined with our work on diary management to maximise each clinician's billing time, have boosted the revenue, profit and growth of the business. This book is the foundation of the success we've seen recently. The Practice with Profit Way works. It's simple, straightforward and will help you to build an engaged, highly motivated team, aligned and working to achieve your health business goals.'

— **Kim Leith**, chartered physiotherapist and clinical lead

'Finally, an open, honest and realistic look at what needs to happen to run a profitable healthcare business. Paul's insight into what goes into running a successful healthcare business from the perspective of the therapist in the consultation room is unique and refreshing. This is a great practical guide that's both easy to read and simple to implement, helping health business owners, leaders and their therapists to maximise revenues profit and growth.'

— **Fiona Moir**, non-clinical director

'Initially, reading this book was a bit of a shock for me – in a good way. I never knew there was so much to learn about being a successful therapist in a profitable health business. Since reading it I feel like I have a much broader understanding of how the business works and the important part I play within it. I'm now starting to think of myself as an expert, a valuable asset, someone who knows what they are talking about. I'm becoming more confident when communicating with patients, establishing goals and "selling" the treatment plan. Following the steps outlined in this book, my patients now understand me better; they have more confidence in me, which leads to increased trust, engagement and commitment, and better outcomes. My patients are very happy with the service I provide, and they're very vocal about it, which brings in a lot more patients to the business.'

— **Hugo Carvalheiro**, clinical lead

Contents

Introduction

Profitable practices

In the health and wellbeing industry, there are a small number of businesses that sell their services at premium prices, enjoy high margins and deliver exceptional value to their ideal customers. What is different about these profitable practices?

- They have a team of motivated, engaged and high-performing practitioners who achieve their financial growth targets

- Their therapists build valuable relationships with patients and enjoy high retention

- Their therapists provide high-value solutions and healthy profits

- They're in demand, with busy diaries full of A-star self-funding patients
- They maximise their return on investment (ROI) in their people and capital assets
- With membership services, they enjoy a recurring-revenue income stream
- They're continuously growing by successfully recruiting like-minded therapists
- Their leaders multiply revenues and profits with minimum stress and maximum freedom

Unprofitable practices

Then there are other health businesses that have been in the industry for years, but are not yet profitable practices:

- They have demotivated, disengaged and poor-performing therapists in their teams
- Miscommunication costs them in lost patients, revenues and profits
- Their therapists find business painful, providing low-value solutions
- They aren't in demand, instead having high cancellation rates
- Their diaries are full of low-revenue or discounted work requiring excessive admin
- They become new-patient focused, wasting marketing money while under-servicing their current patients

- They have a broken transactional business model
- They have high levels of staff turnover with low team morale
- They suffer from a low ROI in their people and capital assets

The leaders of these unprofitable practices are caught in a cycle of despair, a race to the bottom. They're part of a crowd of barely surviving commoditised health businesses providing minimal service at rock-bottom prices, returning low margins in a place where extinction always looms. This cycle of despair is characterised by constant stress on the health-business leader; they're on the treadmill, working as hard and fast as they can, yet their business is going nowhere. This represents a leadership void and business stagnation. At best, they will achieve a poor ROI; at worst, bankruptcy.

It doesn't have to be this way.

My story

At a young age, I learned that getting financially rewarded for helping, serving and solving people's problems is essential to survive and thrive in business. When I was twelve, I crushed my pelvis in a farming accident and, with the help of physiotherapy, I learned to walk again. Don't worry, it only took me a few weeks.

Crucially, it was then that I decided I wanted to become a physiotherapist. Once qualified, I combined my interest in business with my desire to help people and opened my first health business, goPhysio, in 2001.

Over my career, I've been lucky enough to have spent over 30,000 hours in face-to-face consultations, training and coaching patients to recovery. While building my team and growing a health business, I've developed unique insights and solutions to the difficult task of trying to scale a profitable health business. A health business that sells therapists' time and expertise for money. A health business that relies on patient-therapist relationships at its core, the unique thoughts, feelings and behaviours arising from these relationships contributing positively to achieve the financial objectives of the business.

Who is this book for?

This book is for you if you operate or are thinking of opening a health business. It's for you if you have the responsibility for building a highly motivated and productive therapy team that achieves your health business's vision, profit and growth targets.

As a health-business leader and expert therapist, I've learned over the last twenty years that the quickest, easiest, most cost-effective way to maximise profit and growth in any health business is through building valuable patient-therapist relationships in the consultation room. If you have poor patient interaction, broken relationships, disengagement, you'll have poor references and patients will not stay in your network. If you want more patients to stay, you need other tools and techniques that build your network effectively and improve emotional engagement with your health business.

These insights have driven me to develop a unique and easy five-step way to transform your health business for profit and growth, called the Practice with Profit Way. Over the five steps, I reverse a traditional growth model and focus on retention first and foremost.

As health practitioners, we build the foundations of a profitable health business in the consultation room, which is a simple, cost-effective way to grow and scale. We're about the value of the relationship, not the transaction. A patient attending two sessions is a transaction; undergoing a course of treatment, until they've achieved their aims and goals, is a relationship.

This book will outline the methods to help you build a profitable practice, positioned at the top end of your market.

I urge you to go visit my health business website www. goPhysiotherapy.co.uk to see what my team and I have achieved. And you can achieve the same for your health business. Build valuable patient relationships as a fast-track health business growth model to retain and gain A-star self-funding patients, multiplying your revenue, profit and growth.

How to use this book

As you read through the book, I encourage you to approach it with a beginner's mindset – a curious, adaptable, growth mindset. Ask yourself, 'How does this apply to my health business?' and 'How could these five steps help me in my health business?' If you follow my advice, your practitioners will do a great job, your patients will experience great outcomes and you'll reap great rewards.

This book is organised into seven chapters. In Chapter One, we'll discuss the fundamental health-business concepts and principles underpinning the Practice with Profit Way. By applying the 80/20 principle to your health business, you'll learn how to future-proof it by moving the critical 'growth levers' and multiplying your revenues, exponentially growing your profits.

In Chapters Two to Six, we'll cover each of the five steps in the Practice with Profit Way. This follows a patient journey from pain to gain through your health business. In a successful health business, this is also a financial journey. When you do it well, your patients will engage and stay for the whole journey, refer business to you, and your health practice will get financially rewarded. The outcomes are healthy patients and a healthy, profitable business. It's a sustainable journey with referrals into other products or membership services relevant to the journey embedding patients into your business ecosystem for the long term.

- In Step 1, Culture, we focus on maximising your therapist utilisation and health business capacity.

- In Step 2, Connect, we maximise value, equipping you with the tools to build valuable patient-therapist relationships in the consultation room.

- In Step 3, Convert, we focus on the ultimate aim of the initial consultation, which is to maximise patient conversion by introducing a course of therapy as a fundamental starting point in the patient's recovery journey.

- In Step 4, Consult, we'll look at many best-practice techniques to maximise patient consultations through adding value, building engagement and retention. This ensures your therapists guide their patients on a successful recovery journey until they achieve their unique aims and goals.

- In Step 5, Consistent, we focus on a best-practice management and leadership system to build a consistently high-performing therapy team for profit growth and scale.

In Chapter Seven, we will look at the true cost of not implementing the Practice with Profit Way into your health business in terms of lost patients, revenues and profits. We'll calculate the rewards of adopting this approach and identify the opportunities and next steps to quickly and easily achieve your profit goals.

As a health-business leader, by using the Practice with Profit Way, you'll become clear on how to succeed in your primary role of converting your assets into revenue, while minimising expense. You'll be able to start implementing these strategies and grow your health business around retaining and gaining A-star self-funding patients, maximising your profit and growth. When your therapists are doing a great job, your patients will have great outcomes. Healthy patients equal a healthy, profitable business.

Stakeholder success

I'll show you exactly how to achieve this by investing in your people, equipping them with the skills to build valuable, long-term patient-therapist relationships in the consultation room as a quick, valid way to transform your health business for profit and growth. When you commit to these simple steps, you'll smash it, multiplying your profits and growing your practice with less time and more freedom.

Let's get started.

One
The Practice With Profit Way

In this chapter we'll discuss the commercial reasoning under-pinning the Practice with Profit Way. We'll go four layers deep in applying the 80/20 principle to your health business, and unearth the opportunities for exponential revenues, profit and growth. We'll examine the different agendas each stakeholder brings to the consultation room and the common goal to achieve a win-win result. You'll discover how to unlock the profit currently hidden at the core of your health business to produce exponential growth, developing a razor-sharp focus on guiding each patient along a successful journey to recovery while improving outcomes and revenues.

80/20 principle

Being lean is critical for success in business in the modern age. Successfully implementing this approach in your business starts with an understanding of Pareto's law, which is named after an Italian economist Vilfredo Pareto. It is also known as the 80/20 principle which Richard Koch wrote about in his best-selling book of the same name (2007).

The 80/20 principle is a universal law where typically 80% of results flow from 20% of the effort, helping individuals and groups achieve more with less. The key point is not the exact percentages, but rather the maximising of reward with minimal effort that can be applied to almost any scenario.

Here are some examples applied to a health business:

- 80% of your revenue will come from 20% of your health businesses activities, so 80% of the activities your health business performs only contributes to 20% of your revenue

- 80% of your profit comes from 20% of your customers, so 80% of your customers generate only 20% of your profits

For example, if you employ ten therapists, two will generate 80% of the sales and the other eight therapists will only generate 20% of the sales. That means person for person, the first two are sixteen times more effective than the other eight.

Perry Marshall in his prize-winning book *80/20 Sales and Marketing* (2013) explains that understanding the 80/20 principle is just the starting point; the real power to exponentially grow your business and profits comes when you leverage the 80/20 principle focusing on the layers.

The Practice with Profit steps will help you understand the 80/20 principle and the power in its layers to grow, scale and transform your health business.

1. **80/20 Layer 1:** what are the 20% of activities that give 80% of the profit, ie sixteen times the results of the other 80%?

2. **80/20 Layer 2:** what are the 20% of the 20% (4%) of activities that give 250 times the rewards?

3. **80/20 Layer 3:** what are the 20% of the 20% of the 20% (0.8%) of activities that give 4,000 times the results?

4. **80/20 Layer 4:** what are the 20% of the 20% of the 20% of the 20% (0.16%) of activities that give 65,000 times the results?

I've studied and applied this principle to my clinical practice and health business over the last ten years and identified the areas of most value to profit and growth. Layer one starts with an understanding of the growth levers under your control.

80/20 layer 1: growth levers

In the first layer of applying the 80/20 principle towards building a profitable practice, we'll identify the crucial 20% of your health businesses activities that produce 80% of the profits. This starts with an understanding of the opportunities for growth or 'growth levers' in your health business, developing clarity of insight on what levers you can move to achieve your health-business goals. It was a game-changer for me, and I'm confident it will be a game-changer for you.

I've illustrated this concept in the diagram below, bringing it to life with real-world data from my own health business. I'll explain how each constraint affects the ROI on your two biggest expenses: your capital and your people, helping you prioritise which growth levers you should focus on for the most impact and quickest results.

1. **Premises.** The first major barrier to the growth of your health business is your premises: the physical square footage of your health business and its associated capital expense. This is the largest expenditure for a health business and is relatively fixed.

2. **Billable consultation space.** The next constraint is the area or space set aside for billable activities in your health

business, such as consultation rooms, studios and other treatment spaces. Ideally, your premises layout and design should maximise this area. This has a dramatic impact on your revenue and profitability. Unfortunately, it's always less than the whole premises; the question is how to minimise this reduction.

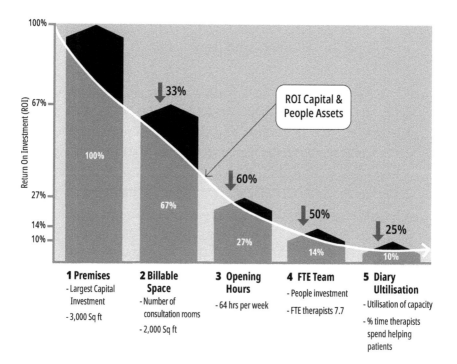

Health business growth levers

The costs associated with this space are fixed, so it's about maximising available billable space to maximise your ROI. At goPhysio, through long-term planning we've had the luxury of purpose designing and building our dream practice. We've minimised non-billable space while maximising the team environment and patient facilities, but it's a fine balance.

3. **Opening hours.** Opening hours are within your control to a degree, but require a careful balance between many factors that affect work/life and retention of your team. Could you:

- Open for longer each day?
- Split shifts between earlies and lates?
- Open on weekends and bank holidays?

It's crucial to involve your team in these discussions and decisions. It improves their awareness of the big picture, the business model constraints and the difficult juggling act of welfare and purpose before profits. It gives your practitioners context and understanding of the importance of positively affecting the levers under their control in their day-to-day roles and responsibilities. Crucially, it helps them sharpen their focus and improves their responsibility for the behaviours they can control in their patient-therapist relationships and performance.

My health business is open five days per week, twelve hours per day, plus four hours on the sixth day, so a total of sixty-four hours per week. Shockingly, this equates to only 40% of the total available hours per week, ie a striking 60% reduction in potential ROI as our capital expenses are fixed and the bills are spread over the full 168 hours per week for fifty-two weeks of the year, regardless of our opening hours.

4. **Number of therapists.** The next major growth lever is your people, denoted by the number of full-time employed (FTE) practitioners you have in your team. This is your second

largest investment after your premises. An important point to note is that I refer to *full-time therapists.*

It never ceases to amaze me that the first thing many health business owners tell me is how many therapists they have working for them. They wear it like a badge, they plaster it all over their website. When I question them, I often find their business consists of ten part-time practitioners doing an odd mix of hours, ultimately equating to three FTEs, so their total therapist number is purely a vanity metric. Without clarity, they're managing chaos: too many people with too little ROI. The number of FTE therapists cuts through the noise; it is a direct measurement of capacity.

At goPhysio we've calculated the maximum number of FTE therapists our health business premises can realistically accommodate. I suggest you do the same, as the reality may be quite different to what you expect. This provides a useful starting point and a realistic target to aim for, then with this book, you'll learn the key elements to developing a winning recruitment strategy to increase the capacity of your health business with aligned and purposeful therapists, maximising revenue, profits, growth and scale.

5. **Utilisation of capacity.** This last lever refers to your therapists' understanding of your business model and ultimately answers this simple question:

'What is the money-making model in our health business?'

For example, a hotel sells room bookings, a restaurant sells table covers, so what is your health business selling? To put it simply, on the balance sheet, you're selling appointment time with your therapists to achieve a patient's result. From a practical health-business leader's perspective, you're interested in:

- The utilisation and percentage occupancy of your therapists' diaries

- The utilisation of the business premises over a day, a week, a year

Diary utilisation directly relates to:

- How much value are your therapists creating and delivering to their patients over the whole course of their recovery journey?

- How much do their patients believe in them and trust them to help them achieve their aims and goals?

- How many patients cancel their appointments with a polite 'I'll look at my diary and get back to you', and then fail to reschedule?

- How many disengage prematurely due to poor outcomes, never to be seen again?

The answers to all those questions are reflected in measuring the utilisation of your individual therapists, your team and health business as a whole.

- Maximise the number of FTE practitioners employed in your health business

- Maximise their capacity or utilisation

Combined, they represent the total time your health business and therapists spend getting paid for doing what you're employing them and they were trained to do: helping patients. By applying the 80/20 principle through the growth levers, you identify the crucial 20% of activities you need to focus on to maximise revenue and profit:

Maximise the number of FTE therapists you have and the time they spend in billable activities, such as one-to-one consultations with patients.

If you move and improve these two levers, the lowest-hanging fruit on the graph, over the next six to twelve months, you'll have the ability to grow your revenue and profits by at least 270%. Maximising the number of therapists in the practice and their utilisation is the highest priority for any health business to maximise ROI in its people and capital assets, the two biggest expenses in the business. As you have specific levels of capacity, maximising utilisation instantly tells you how well your team and business are performing.

The great news is there is a lot you can do to maximise these areas of your health business. I urge you to discuss these growth levers with your therapists and examine how they relate to your business. Invest in your therapists, help them to understand their role in the success of the health business. Develop a clear focus on the important elements that they can control day-to-day with their patients in the consultation room.

Applying this first layer of the 80/20 principle towards building a profitable practice, you'll discovered that 80% of the monetisation, profit and growth opportunities for all health businesses exists with maximising the number of FTE therapists and the time they spend in consultations with patients.

80/20 layer 2: valuable relationships

In layer one, we looked at maximising the number of FTE therapists and the time they spend in one-to-one consultations helping patients, but what is the crucial 20% of activities they need to be focusing on in that time to give 80% of the results? Based on my twenty-four years of clinical and business experience, I've found a major revelation for any health business. This vital activity is:

Building valuable patient-therapist relationships in the consultation room.

If your therapists focus exclusively on this, it will return up to 250 times the results.

When you examine your patient's journey deeply, you'll understand that what goes on in the treatment room – the relationship, the connections – determines the vast majority of your success. Acting on this insider knowledge, you can reverse the traditional business growth model to focus on retaining and gaining your ideal clients through valuable patient-therapist relationships first and foremost. As Royston Guest outlines in his great book *Built to Grow* (2017), a traditional business growth strategy would focus on customer acquisition, monetisation and retention (AMR) in that order.

I've come to realise that in a relationship business, it's quicker and more effective to flip the classic AMR strategy on its head and focus on retention first to dramatically drive revenue, profit and growth. By all means keep doing a little of your current marketing, the usual activities, but don't try to grow your business through marketing investment until you've adopted a repeatable, winning system that consistently builds valuable patient-therapist relationships in the consultation room.

That's a common mistake many health businesses make. If you simply focus your attention on increasing your marketing investment to grow, your therapists will continue to under-service their patients. At best, you'll be managing the mediocre while wasting your marketing money. At worst, you'll be marketing yourself to bankruptcy.

As a health-business leader, you need to understand where the value is in your health business, then focus on this value to exponentially grow your business. When you look under the bonnet of the most successful businesses, you're likely to see an entirely different animal to what you may expect. Take McDonald's for example. When Ray Kroc was asked what business McDonald's was in, he stated that it wasn't in the hamburger business, it was in the real-estate business. As health practitioners, we're not in the health business, we're in the relationship business.

Ultimately for health businesses, the simplest, most cost-effective way to profit and growth comes through giving patients what they want, which is connection and trust in the consultation room. Teach your therapists how to do it right, how to see the potential value of a healthy patient, and to recognise where they can add value to the patient journey, providing great benefits and building a profitable business.

80/20 layer 3: self-funding patients

In layer three of the 80/20 principle, we go deeper and identify what it is about the top 20% of patient-therapist relationships (0.8% of health-business activities) that could return up to 4,000 times the results. Based on my twenty-four years' clinical and business experience, it is without doubt building valuable patient-therapist relationships with high-value A-star self-funding patients. By identifying and shifting your focus to A-star self-funding patients, you'll multiply your profits and growth, transforming your health business and building a profitable practice around your ideal clients.

Strategically target the most profitable segment of your patient database and choose to do business with those patients only. It's important to know your ideal customer. Which segment of your customer base is happy to pay for your therapy services, products and ongoing membership services? To find this out, I suggest you grade each patient on your database from A to D on factors such as:

- **Method of payment:** do they self-fund or pay via health insurance or intermediary medico-legal companies?

- **Rates of payment:** how much are you paid per consultation?

- **Discount:** how much discount are you giving compared with your ideal clients?

- **Administration:** how many resources are involved with servicing this patient segment?

- **Payment terms:** how quickly do you get paid – thirty days, sixty days, ninety days?

- **Resources:** how much time, energy, hassle does it take to service them and get paid?

- **Cancellation rate:** how much do they value your service?

- **Profit:** what's the profit per consultation?

Then I recommend you stop working with the D clients first, replacing them with A clients. Over a few months, when that's working well and you've grown in confidence, stop working with the C clients, again replacing them with A clients. Repeat this process slowly over a six- to twelve-month period and I guarantee you will fill your business with A-star self-funding patients who value your products and services. Your staff will be happier at work, less stressed and hassled, and your revenues will soar. Crucially, you'll be taking the important first steps towards building a profitable practice.

80/20 layer 4: common goal

Layer four of the 80/20 principle highlights the vital 20% in building valuable patient-therapist relationships that will reap 80% of the profit and rewards. This starts with an understanding that your health business, therapists and patients all bring different agendas, wants and needs to the consultation room.

Your therapists want a great place to work, a great salary, freedom and autonomy, purpose, respect and advancement. The vast majority are not interested in the business perspective or the metrics; they just want to focus on their patients, help people recover and achieve their aims and goals.

Patients have many pressures on their energy and time. They have busy lives at home and at work; they're often rushing about and over committed. They're too busy to have health problems. They don't want to be injured or in pain; they want a quick, convenient result.

The health-business leader has many vital needs to cover. They have to implement all aspects of their organisational chart, from sales and marketing to human resources, finances, leadership, strategy and operations, while covering overheads and making a profit.

As a result of these different agendas, without a clearly focused and aligned strategy, the therapists, patients and health-business leaders may all pull in opposing directions, with massive limitations on productivity, profit and growth.

Misaligned strategy

I've spent my career in my own health business studying these differing agendas and discovering the secrets to unlocking the lost opportunities for growth that exist at the core of most health businesses. There's a sweet spot that cuts through all the noise. It represents a problem shared by all stakeholders that if solved will eradicate all of these agendas.

It's one common goal or result that your therapists, patients and health business all want to achieve.

What is this common goal? Introducing your A-star self-funding patients to a successful course of treatment until they achieve their aim of experiencing health and wellbeing transformations.

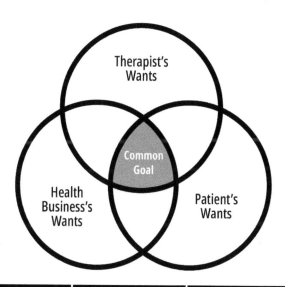

Therapist's Wants	Patient's Wants	Health Business's Wants
- Great numeration	- Quality care	- Self-funding patients
- Autonomy	- Convenient access	- Valuable relationships
- Mastery	- Premium service	- Maximise conversion
- Purpose, helping patients	- Great outcomes	- Engagement and retention
- Work-life balance	- High value	- High utilisation
	- Health transformations	- High-performing team
		- Revenue, profit and growth

Stakeholders' common goal

Successful patient journey

In a successful health business, the patient journey and the commercial journey are intertwined. Patient value and outcomes are the lead. When they're addressed correctly, they will give the desired clinical and financial results.

A successful patient journey is summarised in the graph below.

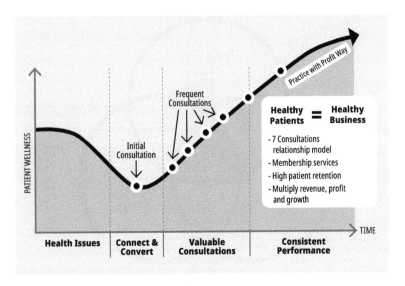

Successful patient journey

1. **Initial consultation.** To be successful, the therapist needs to connect with the patient and identify a problem that there is value in solving, collaborate and engage with the patient to find the solution, and introduce them to a successful course of treatment to achieve their aims and goals.

2. **Frequent consultations.** With frequent consultations, patients experience quick wins and feel the benefits, building

motivation, momentum, engagement, retention, trust and loyalty until they've achieved their aims and goals.

3. Membership. Therapists with clinical mastery tailored to your health business build valuable long-term relationships with A-star self-funding patients. A minimum of 20% of these patients will sign up to your long-term recurring-revenue membership services to achieve further health and wellbeing transformations.

When this is done correctly, the patients stay engaged for the whole journey. They refer business and your health practice gets financially rewarded. If you implement the five steps of the Practice with Profit Way to a high standard, training your therapists in how to capture maximum patient value, it will rapidly increase the spend per head. The outcomes are healthy patients and a sustainable, profitable business.

The beauty of the Practice with Profit Way is that you won't just be reliant on each patient over the short term while they're treated for their illness or injury; you'll create a holistic wellbeing experience and patients will be prepared to pay for a great outcome. This is where a large proportion of the health-business market is missing an opportunity, not having a repeatable system that embeds patients in an ecosystem of services, including membership, spanning the long term.

Unsuccessful patient journey

Some therapists find business painful. They don't understand that a health business needs to be paid for great value and service. They're blind to the many opportunities to add value in the consultation room.

In the initial consultation, therapists often confuse patients about the next steps on their recovery journey by using a purely clinical, evidence-based approach and technical communication style. Confused patients have difficulty seeing the value of the solutions and become indecisive as a result. They then often make poor decisions for their health and wellbeing. This is evidenced by poor conversion rates.

When patients experience poor value, they opt for the low-risk status quo, putting up with long-term suffering and disability. After a broken therapist–patient relationship, the patient disengages with the practice, leading to poor references and no network effect.

When a health business adopts a routine practice of under-servicing its current customers, leading to low engagement and retention, it results in lost revenues, lost profits and a lack of growth. It places high stress on the leader's shoulders along with uncertainty and a lack of control: the downward spiral of despair.

Unfortunately, this scenario is the norm in many health businesses today. In the consultation room behind closed doors, therapist–patient relationships are fracturing in a way that the leaders rarely get to see.

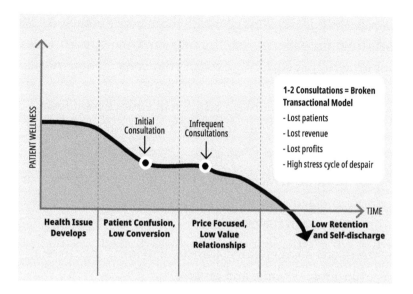

Unsuccessful patient journey

The good news is that when you go four layers deep and highlight the many opportunities for growth and scale that currently exist, with razor-sharp focus you can identify the 0.16% of your health business activities that can give you 65,000 times the rewards. The number-one rule to remember is:

Maximise the number of FTE therapists and the time they spend in consultations building valuable relationships with A-star self-funding patients, leading them into a successful course of treatment until they achieve their aims and goals.

Rather than giving this area of your health business just 0.16% of your energy and focus, I recommend you target and leverage it 100% of the time, exponentially increasing your profits and results. It's simple. When your therapists consistently achieve this goal with the majority of their A-star self-funding patients, you'll understand the opportunities for growth that currently exist in your consultation rooms:

- You don't need more staff. Invest in your current team, equipping them with the skills to build valuable patient relationships.

- You don't need more patients. Instead, take better care of your A-star self-funding patients to retain them and gain more through referrals.

- You don't a larger clinic. Instead, maximise the current utilisation, revenue and profits.

If you want more of your ideal patients to stay, these tools and techniques will improve emotional engagement and build your network effect. As a health-business leader, you'll enjoy the confidence of knowing that all the patients who enter your practice will experience a successful journey to true health transformations. Implementing this process and guiding your patients through their journey from pain to gain will build you a highly profitable health business.

Helping people and being rewarded are not mutually exclusive. In fact, when performed consistently to a high standard, a clear focus on patient experience in the treatment room is a key growth driver and a valid strategy to invest in for any health business. The patients' treatment journey is a financial journey, but this financial element of the health business is often difficult for caring, well-meaning therapists to confront, so you need to be careful with the language you use when discussing your business profit and growth goals with therapists.

I recommend using a business growth model that is aligned to the therapists' purposes of helping people, improving outcomes, engagement and value for patients at every step of their journey to recovery and health transformation. Then when you implement great services into your health business, they will be profitable.

Health-business mastery

The Practice with Profit Way has been devised by a clinical and business expert who has spent twenty+ years in the treatment room, building a health business through valuable relationships, engagement, retention and patient health transformations. Someone who speaks the language of your therapists with empathy and understanding. It has a unique position in the marketplace: it approaches business growth from the patient's and therapist's perspective.

Understanding what's actually going on behind closed doors in the treatment room every hour, day, week, month and year is crucial to the success, profitability and growth of your health business. What's your core service like? Is there any substance to it? Is it sustainable?

All the answers will be outlined in the unique five-step Practice with Profit Way. In this book, I have only included wisdom and advice that is supported by strong data, the latest research and practical tactics that have been successfully tested in the competitive private health industry in the UK today. Since I've refined and adopted this approach, my health business has achieved outstanding success. It's enabled me to:

- Go from being a solo clinician to leading a motivated, engaged and high-performing FTE team of fourteen

- Build a 3,000-square-foot modern freehold premises

- Implement recurring income-generating membership services

- Experience year-on-year growth far in excess of 40%

It's important to be realistic and understand that to build a profitable health business takes time. It takes therapists a decade or two to get good at what they do. Initially, put learning before earning, patience before shortcuts, but with experience, and by applying the 80/20 principle, you can fast-track your way to growth and scale in all health businesses. The process to achieve this is outlined in the five-step Practice with Profit Way, which shows you how you can get maximum profit and growth, whatever stage of development your business is at currently.

Let's read on, starting with the first step in the Practice with Profit Way: Culture. In the next chapter, I'll outline how to develop a winning culture to attract and build an aligned, motivated and high-performing therapy team. It starts with the team leaders and therapists defining and aligning their purpose, culture, vision, values and goals. This closed loop of sustainable business growth based around relationships and helping people is a fast way for any health business to turn its assets into profits without significant financial investment or expense. It's why our teams – the owners, leaders and therapists – are involved in the first place: to facilitate health and wellbeing transformations.

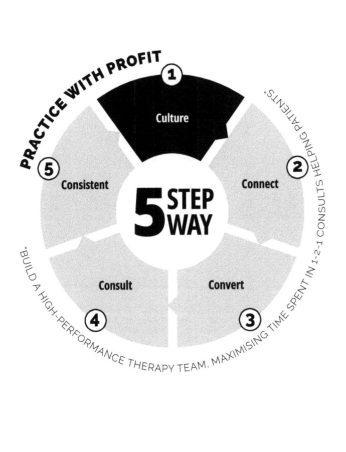

PRACTICE WITH PROFIT

1 Culture

2 Connect

3 Convert

4 Consult

5 Consistent

5 STEP WAY

"BUILD A HIGH-PERFORMANCE THERAPY TEAM, MAXIMISING TIME SPENT IN 1-2-1 CONSULTS HELPING PATIENTS."

Two
Step 1 – Culture

In this chapter, the first step towards health business transformation, we'll focus on how to bring the 80/20 layer one, growth levers, to life.

In Chapter One, we discovered the crucial 20% of activities you need to focus on to maximise revenue and profit:

Maximise the number of FTE therapists and the time they spend in billable consultations with patients.

As you're about to find out, this starts with identifying your health business's purpose. This will help your therapy team adopt value-building behaviours and align them behind your clear and unifying vision. You'll learn practical ways to implement a reward and recognition system to acknowledge and encourage your therapists to live the values and behaviours required to achieve your goals. You'll explore best practice in motivation and behavioural change science to empower your therapists to achieve clinical mastery tailored to your health business, ensuring your recruitment and profiling strategies identify the right people to add to your engaged and productive team. You'll help align your therapists' internal motivations – autonomy, clinical mastery and purpose – with your patients' why.

These are the first vital steps towards your health business's transformation.

Purpose

A business's purpose is its reason to exist, why it does what it does. When you're developing your health business's purpose, it's about finding something that you want to change and ensuring all your therapists and patients have a clear understanding of what this is. It often looks beyond the balance sheet to a broader role for your business in society. What's your reason to exist over and above just making profit? How would you like to contribute to the world?

In his best-selling book, *Building A Story Brand* (2017), author Donald Miller outlines that every great story or vision needs a villain, ie a problem that your company or customers face. An excellent way to recognise the change you want to see in the world that your businesses purpose can achieve is to define your business's enemy, so ask yourself this simple question:

Who or what is the enemy in my business niche?

To help put it into context, in my health business goPhysio, the enemies are:

- Confused patients living an inactive lifestyle due to pain and injury

- Low patient conversion and retention

- Poor outcomes for patients

- A transactional business model that actually loses revenue and profits

Understanding what you're opposed to is a positive process as it helps define your purpose, which is in effect the opposite of your enemy. In the case of goPhysio, this is to *help people live a healthy, active, positive life, pain and injury free.*

Your purpose needs to be believable, true and authentic. It must build trust and link closely with your core business offering. It takes a lot of effort to come up with a great purpose, but it's well worth the effort as it clearly guides all your business decisions thereafter. If something aligns with your purpose, you do it. Likewise, if it doesn't, you don't.

As we have at goPhysio, summarise your business's purpose in a simple, memorable sentence. Team members need to be able to remember it easily so it can act as their guiding light for daily decisions. It needs to be inspiring and motivating, helping therapists make a difference. It needs to align strongly to your team's core beliefs as people, health-business leaders, therapists and patients.

At goPhysio, our core offering is physiotherapy, but since we introduced our great purpose statement, the resultant clarity has enabled us to widen our service offering away from traditional physiotherapy. We now offer a whole ecosystem of products, services and membership packages to our patients, growing from strength to strength. I recommend first and foremost that you define a purpose that fuels the passion within all stakeholders.

Vision

To be profitable and successful for the long term, you need to commercialise your purpose. This you do in a way that resonates with your therapists and patients, so it must be authentic. You achieve this by developing and articulating to your team what Jim Collins in his best-selling book, *Good to Great* (2001), calls a 'big, hairy, audacious goal' (BHAG). This should be a unifying health-business BHAG that your therapists really get behind. It needs to be memorable and clear, avoiding therapist confusion while improving alignment.

So how do you do that?

Firstly, don't make it a financial goal. That's a step too far for most therapists and will turn off your caring, well-meaning health professionals. It can also come across as crass, having a demotivational effect. Believe me, I found that out the hard way, so please learn from my mistakes.

Instead, develop your goal to align with what you'd like your team to achieve in any given day, week, month or year. At goPhysio, our BHAG is to achieve 100,000 patient attendances by a certain date, so although it's not directly linked to a monetary figure, it reflects the factors that make up the financial element of the health business.

Values and behaviours

Once you've defined your health business's purpose and BHAG, it's now about clearly articulating the values and behaviours you'd like your therapists to live to achieve your vision.

Even if you already have a set of health-business values, I recommend you revisit, refine and improve them in the light of what we've discussed so far in this chapter. Develop three to five values you believe it's important for your therapists to adopt to achieve your purpose and vision.

At goPhysio, one example of a value is flexibility of mindset, because:

- The clinical diary regularly changes throughout the day and therapists need to be flexible and adaptable to maintain productivity

- Therapists need to have a growth mindset, open to being taken beyond their traditional clinical focus

- Therapists need to be comfortable with change and widen their perspective, developing clinical mastery tailored to a health business for the benefit of all stakeholders

I'm sure you get the picture: it's about looking at what key behaviours your particular team, marketplace and health business require to achieve your purpose and BHAG.

Create your culture

When you have found your health business's purpose, vision and values, collectively they will define the culture. From the team you hire to the patients who buy from you, your culture will attract like-minded people aligned to your purpose and ultimately your success. As your team grows, your culture will strengthen as people gather around ideas that will change things.

Your purpose and culture must be aligned with the three stakeholders' differing agendas, outlined in Chapter One, to achieve your common goals: growth and success. To transform your health business, start by aligning the whys of each stakeholder:

1. Your health business

2. Your therapists

3. Your patients

Any misalignment will create divisions within the team and negatively affect their performance.

A patient's why

As a health-business leader, understand that your patient's why, their motivations and reasons for coming to see you, is closely linked to your health-business strategy and market positioning, which ultimately determine the patients you're attracting as customers and have a dramatic impact on your health business's profitability, success and growth. You need to have your ideal clients all mapped out: their pains and gains, buying motivations, and your solutions to their wants. This is your value proposition, ie what value your health business is communicating to your ideal clients. It is intrinsically linked to your patients' why, so you need to find the answers to these critical questions:

- Why are the patients here to see us?
- What do they want to achieve?
- What are their aims and goals?

Within the healthcare industry, the number-one reason patients choose and continue with a therapist is because they show they care. Patients are looking for quality of care. They want a connection from one person to another, so throughout all patient interactions, a caring approach is essential. Patients who feel cared for will come back time and time again, ensuring health transformations and health-business success.

At Practice with Profit, we take care of our therapists and patients alike with a cycle of care, which involves all three health business stakeholders taking better care of each other in this specific order:

1. Health business invests in and takes better care of its therapists

2. The therapists are then equipped to take better care of their patients

3. Then, and only then, the patients will take great care of the business, long term

The order is crucial as you cannot expect your therapists to suddenly start taking great care of your patients just because the leadership team has issued a decree. A caring yet commercial culture looks after its therapists by investing in their training and equipping them with the key skills for success in a health business. I don't mean clinical or technical skills; I mean the soft skills, the interpersonal skills like clear communication and professional sales tailored for the consultation room to identify and solve valuable problems that are worth solving.

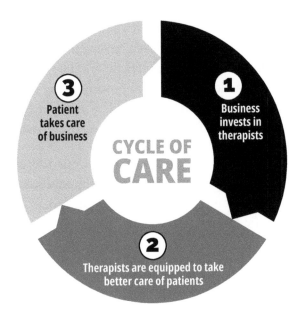

Healthy patients in the context of a healthy, profitable business

These commercial yet caring skills will be a key differentiator for your health business in the future. You cannot expect your patients to engage with your business and offer lifetime value without your therapists first having cared for the patients extensively. That's why purpose, vision and values matter. Build passionate teams who want to make a difference, not just a quick sale. When your team is motivated by a grand purpose, when they understand the change it will make, their performance will soar

Team

The people in your health business are the most important assets you've got. Your role as leader is to turn those assets into revenue and profit while minimising expense.

To build your business, you have to build your team first. Your job as a leader is to build a team aligned with your business's purpose and culture. They need to gather around the founding idea of your business, its purpose and a leader they trust. Trust is a two-way street. For the team to trust the leader, the leader must show the team that they trust them first. Trust is free, it breeds loyalty and brings a team together.

At Practice with Profit, we've identified the easiest and most profitable way to build trust is through our cycle of care approach.

Regardless of what therapists say when leaving a company, they in all likelihood don't leave because of the money or the job. They mostly leave because they're not motivated, they don't feel valued, they aren't engaged. They don't feel part of something that matters to them; they are not being challenged. This will probably be because the business hasn't adequately invested in them and they've stopped learning.

It's your job as leader to create a learning culture that will keep your team members emotionally connected with their hearts in the business. You have to go way beyond training the technical, clinical skills to keep your therapists engaged; it's about the whole person, not just what they do. Encourage therapist self-development; understand their motivations aligned with their purpose and career.

At Practice with Profit, we improve therapists' engagement through the use of motivational interviews. We identify and help therapists understand their internal motivators and drivers, implementing actionable steps in their roles so they become as good as they want to be.

When you invest in the soft skills, you make your therapists feel part of the bigger picture. They realise they're effecting true transformational change in their patients' lives. Send them on self-discovery courses because, as Henry Ford stated, 'The only thing worse than training your employees and having them leave is not training them and having them stay.'

Reward and recognition

When you have developed your purpose, vision and values and identified your culture, articulate them throughout the business clearly and consistently. Demonstrate the behaviours that your teams need to live to achieve your BHAG.

It's vital everyone within the business should 'live' your culture from the top down, but this won't happen on its own. It's the team leader's role to recognise and reward as and when this happens in real-time, making sure it's consistent and authentic. Culture is not a fad.

To embed your values and guide behaviours deeply within your health business as 'the way we do things here' takes organisation, consistency and effort. You need to implement a clear and simple communication system to give positive, timely feedback on all the vital day-to-day therapist activities and behaviours that contribute to achieving your BHAG.

At goPhysio, we have a clear focus on living the values towards achieving our 100,000 attendance goal:

- What percentage of their time at work do therapists spend face-to-face with patients, helping them achieve their aims and goals?

- Do therapists follow great diary management principles, maximising occupancy where possible?

- Do they ring back promptly when a patient has an enquiry and wants to speak to a therapist before booking an appointment?

- What do they do when someone cancels? Do they ring them back as soon as possible to see how they are and offer further guidance and help?

Many small day-to-day actions go towards achieving your purpose and BHAG, so make sure you give timely recognition in the form of thanks. There are a wealth of software platforms in the HR space that have great, simple 'Thanks' systems.

Customer Champion

" Hi Hugo,

This is to say thank you for being a customer champion last month and achieving your customer engagement target of 88%. Out of the thirty-three new patients you assessed last month, only four attended three consultations or fewer. This demonstrates that you are connecting with patients, and identifying and solving high-value problems. Patients are engaged; they trust and believe in you as the solution. You are walking the walk – great effort! "

Hugo received thanks from
Paul Baker - Mon, 04 Mar 2019

Thank you – walking the walk

Therapist motivation

The next layer of building a profitable practice is to develop an understanding of your therapists' individual intrinsic motivators. What's their purpose and passion? Why did they become therapists? Are their motivators being fulfilled in their current role?

As outlined by Clive Steeper and Sue Stockdale in their book *Motivating People in a Week* (2016), motivation can be simply defined as the reason for an action. It relates to the desire, want or need for an individual to behave in a particular way.

The motivation of your team can be likened to the health of your business. It is dynamic; it changes over time and needs to be regularly monitored and reviewed.

It's the team lead's responsibility to identify and react to these changes. The team lead develops employees who contribute to the financial objectives of the health business, so they need to be committed to increasing and maintaining the motivation of their team members. It's definitely not a fad.

If you're a visionary leader, if you're involved in planning and thinking about the next two to three years' growth of your health business, you'll need to interweave therapist motivation with performance management. You need to be continuously planning ahead, having a full understanding of what your therapists want to achieve as individuals at work and helping them do it. This will build a strong, engaged and high-performing team.

There is an overwhelming amount of intrinsic and extrinsic factors that can affect the motivation of individuals at work.

Thankfully, Daniel Pink in his best-selling book, *Drive* (2011), gives great insight and practical tips on how to improve employee motivation. He explains that once you pay your people enough to take the distraction of salary off the table, it's about satisfying three critical factors: autonomy, mastery and purpose.

At Practice with Profit, we have adopted this approach, tailoring it for the health and wellbeing industry and weaving it throughout the Practice with Profit Way. This approach builds on the health business's, therapists' and patients' purpose, and we've found that it's a great foundation on which to boost your team's motivation and performance.

Motivational gap

It's important to give your therapists some time out of their day job to attend seminars and workshops; to get involved in a dedicated programme to explore their motivations, understand themselves better, use their brainpower and gain some critical self-development. At Practice with Profit, we create an environment that encourages motivation with investing in and caring for people at its core. This process starts after you've clearly defined your health business's purpose, BHAG, vision and values – your culture.

Then team leaders need to use this process to assess the motivational gap:

1. Firstly, identify the current intrinsic motivators of each individual therapist. Everyone's unique mix of motivations changes over time.

2. Secondly, assess how well each individual is being fulfilled in their current role. This will highlight the motivational gap.

Aim to understand the therapist. Help them define their motivators and facilitate alignment with the overall business purpose.

When the intrinsic motivators of a therapist are misaligned with their role and responsibilities, this disconnection can impact on performance, patient experience and outcomes. Achieving alignment sounds difficult on paper, but in reality, it is relatively straightforward.

At Practice with Profit, we recommend you do this in the form of quarterly personal-development interviews, best-practice coaching and interviews to unearth the therapist's intrinsic motivators. This is best done with the help of a specialist coach. These motivators might be expertise development, being more creative or feeling valued, to name a few.

Once you have accurately assessed and understood your therapists' motivators, the next step is to ensure that they're being fulfilled in their role. Then provide an open exchange between therapist, coach and team lead to build the intrinsic motivators into the practical aspects of the therapists' role. For example, the team lead could ask, 'If your desire to be creative was being fulfilled in your role, what would your role look like?'

Alternatively, if developing expertise in their role was an important motivator, explore opportunities for the therapist to do this. It could involve them specialising in a niche therapy while developing a new service and building a viable revenue stream.

Ultimately, as a health-business leader, you don't have the luxury of satisfying therapists' motivators carte blanche. There has to be a financial strategy behind it with a clear focus on the patient, the service and the solution. The solution needs to be therapist led so they can develop ownership, which improves intrinsic motivation.

You're likely to be amazed how simple the solutions are when you just ask.

Approximately 30% of therapists exhibit altruism. Among the vast majority of therapists we profile at Practice with Profit, one of the strongest motivators is to make a difference. They want to have meaning and purpose in what they do, which is great. It's a prerequisite to being a successful, caring, helpful therapist, but one-third of therapists place financial reward as their lowest motivator.

This presents a massive internal conflict to therapists working in a health business as their internal dialogues can sabotage their success. They believe the wellbeing of others is equally, if not more important than their own.

Without a validated, repeatable motivational system, these altruistic therapists are actually the most damaging in your health business. They make personal and professional sacrifices to help people. The only problem is they are also unknowingly sabotaging their patients' and health business's success.

For example, they'll come out with things such as:

- 'I know you're only 60% better, but let's not make another booking. Continue with the exercises and see how you get on. Just call me if you need me.'
- 'Don't worry, if you feel a bit better and think you don't need to see me, just ring up and cancel. It's fine.'
- 'Email me if you're worried and I'll teach you how to self-treat for free. I so want to help you that I'm happy to give it away. I get paid anyway, thanks.'

In other words, therapists are giving away their time, knowledge, experience and expertise, which adds no financial value to your business whatsoever. Can you picture past and present colleagues who just don't get it in this way?

Behavioural change

Changing people's behaviour has a complex filter. To manage behavioural change successfully, in either therapists or patients, you have to fit in with their purpose and meaning. If there is a mismatch, it will never happen. Your therapists will never change, your patients and business will never change.

As Dr Steve Peters explains in his award-winning book *The Chimp Paradox* (2012), people respond to perceived threats, or change, by trying to stay safe. Change is essentially a cost-benefit analysis, as people want to avoid pain while looking to do things that provide benefit:

- Therapists will only change their practice and behaviour, layering the commercial with the clinical and developing mastery tailored to a health business, if there is a pay-off. For example, a great place to work, a fair salary, freedom and autonomy, purpose in their work, making a difference.

- Your ideal patients are cash-rich, but time-poor. They have busy lives with many commitments. Despite the best intentions, they often find themselves cancelling appointments, derailing their progress. They will only commit fully to completing a course of treatment until they achieve their aims and goals if your therapists repeatedly answer one crucial question for them: 'What's in it for me?'

Change must be holistic. The complete human being is where the impact is, so change has to fit in with the construct of the therapist's entire life. That's why interpersonal skills are key to clinical mastery.

To effectively change, your therapists need to understand:

- What's in it for them?
- What's the pay-off?
- What's the benefit to change?

When you're adopting behavioural strategies with the people in your health business, follow best-practice principles that have been successfully stress tested in the health industry. The changes you're planning should be realistic and achievable, as poorly implemented, unpredictable change can be stressful for therapists.

Let's bring it to life with a real-world scenario. Altruistic therapists self-sacrifice, it's a fact, but unbeknown to them, by doing so they're sacrificing their patients' and health business's success. Any change for them must be holistic, aligned to their purpose and motivators for success. Through motivational interviews and practical tools, we identified that one particular therapist's key motivations were:

- **Primary motivators:** meaning, making a difference, improving patients' quality of life
- **Secondary motivators:** opportunities to learn, developing expertise and specialism in a subject, sharing expertise
- **Lowest motivator:** material and financial reward

The primary and secondary motivators in isolation are laudable; this therapist would make a great addition to any team. The issue is that material or financial reward is their lowest motivator, which creates an internal conflict. Studying the day-to-day actions and behaviours of an altruistic therapist, analysing his key performance indicators (KPIs), we at Practice with Profit identified a worrying trend:

- A consistently higher than usual cancellation rate (20%)
- A large percentage of his patients (40%) only attending one or two appointments

In other words, he was under-servicing at least 40% of his patients. They were disengaging prematurely, not achieving their aims and goals, and still suffering in the marketplace.

When you implement a repeatable, validated system for identifying your therapists' internal motivators, you can help your altruistic therapists see the error of their ways. Then you can implement training and coaching to improve their mindset, communication and sales skills.

This process starts with structured coaching conversations around what would motivate and trigger the therapists to live the values and behaviours for a more effective and profitable health business. In the example we've been using, it is much more effective to challenge the altruistic therapist on their secondary motivators of expertise, as you too want their patients to get great outcomes. Paint a picture of what expert therapists in a health business achieve:

- They identify and solve meaningful problems for their patients
- They add value at every touchpoint, engaging and motivating their patients
- Their patients successfully complete their treatment programmes until 100% better
- Their patients achieve great outcomes, and a large percentage transfer to membership services

Then explain, referencing the therapists' statistics from case reviews, that they have clearly not been delivering expertise with a certain percentage of their caseload. Through coaching techniques, explore the opportunities for them to change, referencing their secondary motivators to reduce the impact of their altruistic tendencies. You could ask:

- How could the therapists better use their expertise to help all their patients achieve their goals?

- What's the best thing they could change to achieve greater conversion and success?

- What support do they need from the leader and team to achieve this?

Interestingly, therapists rarely request more technical courses or training, which is what most health businesses focus on.

When you've correctly identified your therapists' motivators and implemented a sound coaching programme to bring out the best in them, it's transformational. A health business with engaged, motivated therapists, living their purpose through their patient relationships in the consultation room, developing clinical mastery, becomes a powerhouse of performance. All the therapists in your team will be major assets to your health business, ensuring you'll survive and thrive in the future.

Recruitment profiles

Once you've identified your business's culture and got your current team behind it, it's time to develop a winning recruitment strategy to maximise the number of like-minded FTE therapists in your health business. At Practice with Profit, we have a recruitment system to identify the right therapists aligned with our purpose and vision, ensuring we build a highly motivated and productive therapy team. Our recruitment process is covered further in our blogs at www.practicewithprofit.com/blog.

There are a number of profiling methods available, each approaching recruitment from a different angle. Some take a purely scientific approach, others are a little more esoteric, but only using one aspect of a person's make-up can be misleading. It is important to understand that the function of profiling is not to replace good interview techniques. A trusted method of profiling will, however, complement an interviewer's opinion and either reinforce their views or uncover facets of a candidate's personality that remained hidden in the interview situation. It is an invaluable second opinion, providing direction on developing focused interview questions.

As a health-business owner, you don't need me to tell you that employing the wrong person can have disastrous results, affecting the team around them and having a negative impact on efficiency, morale and profits. The right profiling system as part of your approach to recruiting talent provides an almost foolproof way to avoid costly mistakes and ensure that the right people are in the right positions.

The true value of the profiling tool we use at Practice with Profits comes in the form of a report and telephone call, during which we discuss the candidate's temperament, aptitude, attitude, occupational preferences and suitability for their profession, role and the business. The results show not only what kind of work they would be good, or not so good, at, but more importantly what sort of work they would enjoy.

This open and frank discussion about the candidate's suitability can cover various angles, for example:

- **Potential duration of tenure.** In the last three years, only one employee whom we've used this system to recruit has left, and that was due to unavoidable personal issues.

- **Potential miscommunication issues.** Sometimes a candidate's natural communication style is better suited to a research post rather than a customer-facing therapist role in a fast-paced health business.

- **Aptitude score.** If they're too bright, the candidate may have difficulty staying satisfied in the post and will use the role as a stepping-stone, moving along quickly to the next big thing in their career.

- **Responsibility.** The candidate might be likely to flit from task to task, from project to project, never completing anything. They may have difficulty remaining in one location, always looking to spread their wings.

Here's an example of a conversation I may have with a profile partner:

PROFILE PARTNER: Paul, do you want to train this candidate?

PAUL: As a long-term team member, yes, but not as a short-term one as it takes at least six months and a lot of resources for new team members to start performing well in our health business.

PROFILE PARTNER: Then he's not your ideal profile. Don't do it. He's got an independent streak and typically won't stay anywhere more than eight to twelve months. If you're desperate for a warm body in a seat for the short term, then OK. Otherwise don't touch him.

PAUL: Oh thanks, I thought he was the one. He performed so well on the phone.

PROFILE PARTNER: He would. This type of profile is highly intelligent, great initially with people, but after a couple of months the cracks will show.

PAUL: Thanks again for saving us a lot of hassle and expense, much appreciated.

There you have it. An expert cutting through to the heart of the issue gives insight and perspective that can save your health business hundreds of thousands of pounds per annum in poor recruitment decisions, as well as saving it from:

- High training costs
- Damage to culture and team morale
- Poor patient outcomes
- Lost patients, revenues and profits

It is crucial to keep in mind that there are no bad profiles, just incompatibility with the roles and culture of your health business. You're not attempting to clone your top performers; rather, you need variety in the team, so celebrate the differences. But do profile your top performers and identify common traits that are aligned with your health business's vision and culture.

At goPhysio and Practice with Profit, there is a high bar to join the teams. When we make the decision on a candidate, it's based on a green light from both our profiling and our recruitment process, which gives us and our clients the utmost confidence that we get our new hires right 99% of the time.

Tangible takeaways

In this chapter we've outlined the many parts to transforming your health business's culture. The ultimate aim of the commercial yet caring culture is to maximise the number of FTE therapists and the time they spend in billable consultations, helping patients. It's the first vital step to multiplying your profits and growing your practice.

I'm a realist and I understand it will take a long time to implement all these elements to a high degree, so I've broken them down into seven tangible takeaways. Choose between one and two takeaways to introduce into your business per quarter as part of your best-practice performance management system, which we'll explore further in Chapter Six.

1. **Purpose.** Define your health business's purpose. This is its reason to exist beyond just making profit.

2. **Vision.** Communicate your purpose in terms of helping people, therapist productivity and business goals in one simplified, clear and unifying goal.

3. **Values.** Articulate the values and behaviours your therapists should 'live' to achieve your health business's purpose and vision.

4. **Team.** As a health-business leader, your job is to build a high-performing therapy team that achieves the objectives of your business, ensuring you can sell at premium prices and enjoy high profit margins by delivering exceptional service to a large list of ideal customers.

5. **Reward and recognition.** Living the value-building behaviours needs to be consistent and authentic; it's not a fad. Notice and reward the small day-to-day actions that go towards achieving your BHAG. Give timely recognition in the form of thanks through a range of software platforms in the human resources space.

6. **Therapist motivation.** As a health-business leader, it's your responsibility to identify your therapists' intrinsic motivators and react to any changes on a regular basis. Assess their motivational gap through interviews and implement a coaching plan based around best-practice behavioural change science. Take money off the table and satisfy their autonomy, mastery and purpose needs to build a strong, engaged and high-performing team.

7. **Recruitment profiles.** A best-practice approach to a winning recruitment strategy is to profile your top performers and identify common traits that are aligned with your health business's vision and culture. This provides an invaluable second opinion and direction on developing focused interview questions. Then base your successful recruitment decisions on a green light from your profiling tool and your in-house recruitment process. It ensures you'll get your new hires right 99% of the time.

You've taken your first step into the Practice with Profit Way by exploring how implementing a caring yet commercial culture helps build an aligned, motivated and productive therapy team. In the next step, Connect, we'll dive deep into layer two of the 80/20 principle: building valuable patient–therapist relationships in the consultation room.

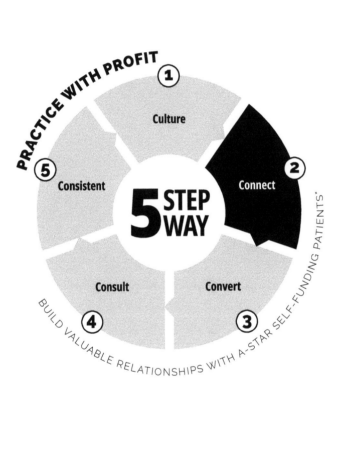

PRACTICE WITH PROFIT

① Culture

② Connect

5 STEP WAY

⑤ Consistent

④ Consult

③ Convert

BUILD VALUABLE RELATIONSHIPS WITH A-STAR SELF-FUNDING PATIENTS"

Three
Step 2 – Connect

In this chapter, looking at your second step to health-business transformation, we'll focus on how to bring the second layer of the 80/20 principle to life by identifying the value in the patient consultation that gives you 80% of the results. This vital activity is building valuable patient-therapist relationships in the consultation room. It is the foundation on which to build long-term relationships.

The first major touchpoint your patients have with your therapists along their journey to recovery starts with likeability, open questions and connecting. In this step of the Practice with Profit Way, we'll look at the practical tools and techniques your therapists can use to quickly connect and assess their patients' why, identifying high-value problems that are worth solving. We'll highlight the nuggets of information your therapists need to discover to develop remarkable solutions and successful conversion conversations.

We'll explore your therapists' interpersonal, relationship and communication skills to connect, unearth and identify value: the cornerstone for a long-term mutually beneficial patient-therapist partnership.

Ultimately, we're in a relationship business, and what goes on in the treatment room – the relationship, the connections – will determine your health-business success.

Miscommunication

Developing the soft interpersonal skills (communication and relationships) is a vital but usually overlooked element in achieving true clinical mastery tailored to a health business. If a therapist develops these skills to a high degree, they will dramatically improve their patients' decision-making process, engagement, outcomes and business success.

Unfortunately, many therapists have a natural tendency towards a confusingly technical communication style. I've repeatedly observed therapists in the face of complex problems lapse into unclear, ambiguous messages. They're honestly confused with which approach to take.

Therapists are primed for clinical practice; it's their sole focus. They ask their patients questions while formulating a scientifically reasoned diagnosis and evidence-based treatment plan. This purely clinical focus leads to a technical communication style at the expense of developing equally important interpersonal skills. They're too mentally preoccupied, ticking off checklists, satisfying the scientific justification, to truly understand and empathise with the patient's perspective. They're bogged down in the technical, while convincing themselves they're providing a great patient experience. They're too busy listening with the intent to reply with more clinical questions, rather than listening purely to explore and understand.

All the while, the patient's becoming confused, unclear of the next steps. Confused patients make poor decisions regarding their welfare, which isn't good for business.

Technical knowledge, experience and skills are great and to be applauded. Therapists should strive to be the best they can be technically, but this is rarely the issue when they're trying to improve patient engagement and deliver great outcomes. The issue is that the technical aspect of the consultation is their sole focus.

Therapists need to take responsibility for what their patients hear, what they understand and the messages they leave the consultation with. This reminds me of a fundamental guiding principle in my career as a therapist, health business owner and leader, from a quote most often attributed to Robert McCloskey (and discussed in Zieg, 1980):

> 'I know that you believe you understand what you
> think I said, but I'm not sure you realise that what
> you heard is not what I meant.'

The pitfalls of miscommunication in all patient interactions are summed up in this one powerful sentence. It has had a big impression on me throughout my career, enabling me to cut through the noise and get to the heart of most matters quickly.

Cause

In all health businesses, there are common reasons for miscommunication:

- There is an absence of training, coaching and direction from the leaders. The therapists don't know how to tailor their language to fit a health relationship business to improve patient motivation, outcomes and health transformations.

- In the absence of clear leadership, therapists will default to the purely evidence-based (and mistaken) belief that 'If I study more on my clinical knowledge and skills, I'll be a great therapist'.

- Therapists honestly don't realise that patients interpret their language as unsure, unconfident, ambiguous messages. At times, they may think their words are a bit vague and waffly, but tragically they don't know what else to say.

- Therapists lack the confidence and conviction to commit, afraid of peer pressure and coming across as too salesy. Unfortunately, they take the safe but ineffective middle ground, watering down their recommendations with maybes and possibilities. I guarantee this is the communication style of your poorest performing therapists.

Cost

Not training your therapists in high-level interpersonal communication and relationship skills can cost your health business hundreds of thousands of pounds per annum. If your therapists have not been trained in these interpersonal skills, I guarantee inconsistency throughout all aspects of your health business, leading to:

- Low patient retention: at least 50% of your patients will disengage in three consultations or fewer
- Poor patient outcomes
- Lost revenues, profit and growth

If this is happening in your health business, your team leaders and therapists need to be honest with you and face up to the fact that you're not really helping your patients in a valuable way. Essentially, your practice is part of the problem and not the solution.

Solution

Communication in the high-tech modern world is mostly automated and impersonal. In contrast, in a private health business, your service is formed around a lengthy personalised interaction. It's structured in a way that therapists spend one-to-one time with patients, building interpersonal relationships.

This is a highly positive and future-proofing feature of the health industry. Empathetic therapists who build strong patient-therapist relationships, identifying and solving high-value problems, will have the competitive and economic edge in the coming decades. Your people give your business its single most powerful edge, so developing your therapists' ability to get others to like them, trust them and buy from them is imperative.

Interpersonal skills

At Practice with Profit, we focus on developing the interpersonal skills that enable therapists to quickly connect with their patients to uncover and solve high-value problems. We have a proven system called the Patients' Charter that all therapists follow in their initial patient consultations, drawing on my 30,000 hours of clinical practice. It outlines the key touchpoints in the patients' journey while they're in face-to-face consultations with their therapists.

The Patients' Charter is a system to help guide your patients from their health problems to recovery, built on the insight that patients are assessing your therapists as much as your therapists are assessing them. It requires these common patient questions to be answered in a relaxed, conversational style:

- Am I in the right place?
- What's wrong with me?
- How can you help?
- Will I get back to my aims and goals?
- How long will it take?
- What's the commitment?
- What if I do nothing?

Answering these questions in a clear, positive and relaxed manner helps patients get one step closer to achieving their aims and goals.

Patient understanding

What message do your patients leave their consultations with?

- Maybe this solution will work?
- It might help?
- Hopefully it will improve things?

I've sat in consultations and actually counted how many times therapists have used unclear, ambiguous messages. On average, it's twenty times per consultation. When your patients leave your health business with these messages in their head, what would you expect them to do?

They're at substantial risk of premature disengagement and poor outcomes.

This is a significant factor in the difficulty of scaling patient-therapist relationships and growing your health business: the lack of clear, consistent, confident, positive messages in the consultation room. This statement is not theoretical; it is based on hard evidence I've witnessed countless times in health businesses.

When I start working with a therapist, regardless of their experience, first I work on their interpersonal skills. They're the easiest to improve and highly cost effective with a great ROI, so they're the quick wins that build momentum and success for all.

Training interpersonal skills starts with the understanding that most of your patients are non-medical laypeople, while your therapists are qualified health and wellbeing experts. Your therapists need to communicate in a clear, focused manner so their patients leave with the correct messages and make the best decisions for their health and wellbeing.

Firstly, highlight the habits, hang-ups, blind-spots and weaknesses in the therapists' interpersonal skills that are barriers to their patients' recovery. Educate them on how these barriers limit their success, reducing the effectiveness of their message and ultimately the outcomes for:

- Patients in terms of engagement and health transformations
- The therapists themselves in terms of purpose, job satisfaction, clinical mastery, growth and development
- The health business in terms of patient retention, revenue, profitability and growth

Your therapists need to realise that patients don't act on what they're told; they act on what they hear and understand. The aim is repetitive, clear messaging relative to each patient's unique situation, spoken in a meaningful way they can easily understand. This ensures the patients know that the therapist can help them achieve their aims and goals.

Clear communication

Experienced therapists are not exempt from these miscommunication issues. Even when I shadow therapists who have been in the business for twenty+ years, I see the same communication issues at play. They use a lot of 'white noise', confusing their patients by discussing the technical features of a product or service. Patients aren't interested in the service's features; they want to know about the service's benefits and how it matches their wants emotionally.

To put it simply, you don't know what you don't know. In academic training circles, this is called being unconsciously incompetent in a particular skill. As you learn a new skill, you advance through the four stages of learning:

1. **Unconscious incompetence:** you're unaware of what you don't know

2. **Conscious incompetence:** you're becoming aware of what you don't know

3. **Conscious competence:** you're learning, but performing the skill takes concentration

4. **Unconscious competence:** the skill is second nature

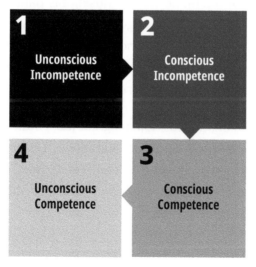

The learning matrix

This approach shows that experience is not everything. Therapists don't need years of experience to be effective with their patients. By quickly up-skilling your therapists in the interpersonal skills to connect with their patients, you can ensure that even recent graduates can soon become productive and successful enough to be a positively contributing team member.

CASE STUDY

Miscommunication happens all the time in patient-therapist relationships. A recent example I observed was with Mark.

Despite the fact that Mark had been qualified for three years and had worked in other health businesses, I found that he had a lot to learn. When I first started working with him, he was confusing his patients with his high-level technical language. He never stopped to consider that they were non-medical people; he believed he was simplifying his language and assumed they understood him and trusted him.

In his opinion, he was doing a great job, getting people better in two to three consultations. Unfortunately, feedback from patients told a different story. They had taken themselves off his lists and gone elsewhere for a solution to their problems.

Throughout our training and coaching programme, I improved Mark's self-confidence by helping him to develop a clearer communication style. We used simple messages that were aligned with his natural style of communication.

With focused training, Mark rapidly progressed his interpersonal skills to consciously competent. In follow-up consultations, he has developed consistent performance, regularly repeating these aligned key messages. With perfect practice, he'll progress to unconscious competence.

Thanks to Mark's focus on repeating clear, simple messages, his patients have no doubts about the benefits he offers. They understand that he will provide the solution to their problem and the difference he can make, so they can now make much better decisions for their welfare, following him on the journey he is expertly trained to take them on. As a result, he is solving valuable problems and improving patient outcomes, helping them achieve their health and wellbeing aims and goals.

Now Mark understands this approach, he's becoming very successful and his patients happily reward him for it with loyalty and trust.

It takes years to train the clinical skills, so optimising the interpersonal skills is a great way to commercialise all your therapists' skills and unlock the growth hidden in the patient-therapist relationships. From day one, it's about the interpersonal skills, the communication and relationship skills, the messages your patients leave the consultation with.

This approach becomes even more effective and valuable with experienced team members tapping into their excellent clinical skills, unlocking rapid growth by altering their mindsets from a purely clinical focus to encompassing the whole health-business ethos. The Practice with Profit Way combines confident clinical abilities with a clear, positive voice in the consultation room, leading patients into a successful course of treatment for the benefit of all.

Understanding the patient's why

A critical factor in determining the success of the initial consultation is the degree to which your therapists gain a clear understanding of their patient's why. What's the patient's reason for being there? What are their health aims and goals?

The prime motivator for patients is to avoid a pain point in one way or another. They want to do things that provide benefit and alter their life state, and they're in the consultation room as their problem is relevant to the therapist's expertise. Any change a patient successfully makes needs to fit in with the construct of their entire life. If there is a mismatch, it will never happen.

When a patient is confronted with change, they almost always return to these questions:

- What's in it for me?
- What's the big pay-off?
- What's are the benefits to change?

Patients willingly commit to a programme and attend appointments if there is a pay-off. Often when patients don't commit fully to a treatment programme and disengage prematurely with their therapist, it's because miscommunication has come into play and they don't perceive any pay-off. Essentially, the patient doesn't experience the benefits or see the value in change.

At Practice with Profit, to help therapists unearth a patient's why and effect positive behavioural change, we've simplified the interpersonal skills required to connect into this process:

- First impressions

- Open questions

- Emotive listening

- Avoid interruptions

- Buying emotions

- Patient motivations

Let's explore each of these critical elements of the patient's initial subjective assessment.

First impressions

The process of connecting starts with first impressions. To develop positive first impressions, your therapists need to do the simple stuff, the marginal gains, such as:

- Introduce themselves with positive language and a handshake, or whatever's natural

- Meet and greet the patient formally in reception
- Chaperone them to the treatment room
- Be professional, friendly and smiling
- Be punctual, or apologise if they're slightly late, which shows they care, respect and value their patient's time
- Be likeable

Jeb Blount, a people and sales expert, is a master in developing likability through a smile. He explains in his award-winning book, *People Buy You* (2010), that ultimately people do not buy from someone they don't like, and the best way to be likeable is to smile. He points out that smiling is a communication tool across all cultures and societies which instantly puts people at ease. As such, smiles are extremely valuable in a health business, creating great first impressions and a relaxed, caring environment.

Don't leave anything to chance in the first impressions your therapists give. Scripts can improve consistency of performance, ensuring they guide their patients on their recovery journey from the get-go.

Here is a simple example of a script to generate a great first impression:

THERAPIST: Hi, I'm Louise, your podiatrist. Pleased to meet you.

Therapist escorts the patient to the treatment room, involving them in small talk focused on understanding their health problems and concerns.

THERAPIST: Have you ever been to see a podiatrist before?

If the answer is no:

THERAPIST: Then I'll explain everything we'll be doing today.

If the answer is yes:

THERAPIST: Oh, when was that? Was it for the same issues or something different?

The therapist lubricates the natural conversation, breaking the ice, then explains what's going to happen in that first session, guiding the patient on their first steps from pain to gain.

Open questions

When your therapists are connecting with people to help them achieve their aims and goals, questions will be the most important things they'll use. Asking open questions is something that most therapists are already highly skilled in – they can direct the conversation towards a clinical diagnosis. At Practice with Profit, we build on this expertise and broaden the therapist's perspective to include the assessment of their patient's why: their motivators, their story.

To understand the patient's story, the therapist asks open questions (ie questions that cannot be answered with a yes or no) and listens to the answers. It's also crucial to avoid long, rambling conversations, which don't work in a health consultation as therapists don't have a vast amount of time at their disposal. It's important to balance between open questions and listening, using targeted questions to guide the patient back or probe in a specific direction to unearth their emotive cues. A therapist provides as much affirmation as possible with positive fillers that lubricate the conversation, such as 'Great, that's interesting, tell me more', then summarises statements back to the patient to make sure they have understood exactly what the patient meant. Therapists need to identify the emotional factors at play, which is sometimes a painful spot for patients. They may be attached to the story their ill health provides, so therapists have to explore a deep layer of internal dialogue to help them recognise who they could become. It's vital to include their future self in their vision, discussing what is in it for the patient in laymen's terms. If your therapists want to unearth meaningful problems and effect patient transformations, they must press on the sore spot where most growth occurs.

It's important your therapists start this process as early in the subjective assessment as possible to give themselves plenty of time to explore the finer points and build a holistic patient story. The expert therapist explores various lines of enquiry, allowing the patient to speak their mind by asking questions such as:

- So, what's the problem?
- How can I help?
- Can you tell me more about how this problem started?
- How has it affected you to date?
- How is this problem affecting you now?
- What would you like to be able to do?

Ultimately, the therapist is getting the patient to paint a picture of their future selves without their problem.

Sometimes, to fully understand the costs versus benefits from the patient's perspective, it's just as useful to assess:

- What do they want to avoid?
- What don't they want to see in future versions of themselves?
- What are the ramifications of doing nothing, of not committing to the solution?

From the start of the initial consultation, your therapists need to be identifying the key issues and the best-fit solution. Within the first ninety seconds of the consultation, they are focusing on building a long-term relationship that will achieve the patient's aims and goals.

Here's an example:

THERAPIST: I can see from your front sheet that you'd like to find out what the problem is and get some advice, is that right?

PATIENT: Yes.

THERAPIST: Well that's the minimum we'll be doing today. Let me explain: we're going to assess your problem in detail with lots of questions and tests. I'll then explain my findings, the diagnosis and prognosis, outline a treatment plan including how many sessions you'll need, the frequency, the different treatments and techniques, and any other products or services that would get you back to your aims and goals quickly if you followed them. How does that sound?

Emotive listening

Listening could be defined as the weakest link in all human interactions. It's hard to tune out of our own thoughts and agenda for long enough to really listen and understand another person, but the better your therapists are at asking questions, the less they'll need to say and the more listening they'll need to do. If your therapists make the commitment to give their patients their complete attention and really listen, your business will prosper.

But true understanding requires them to listen to the messages beneath their patients' words. This helps your therapists to absorb what's being said and, crucially, what's not being said.

In the consultation process, there is always a subtext to the conversation. An expert therapist can read the subtext – the verbal and non-verbal cues, the emotive words, the language the patient uses to describe how their health problems are affecting them on an emotional level – to flesh out their understanding.

Avoid interruptions

A crucial component to listening involves being sensitive and knowing when not to talk. When less confident therapists unearth emotional cues, often they'll be tempted to fill any pauses with closed clinical questions in an attempt to regain control. As a clinical coach and mentor, I've witnessed therapists unknowingly unearth gems of internal dialogue, but they're usually oblivious, not listening, preoccupied with formulating the next question or reasoning the diagnosis.

The expert therapist is mirror-like, demonstrating great coaching skills, reflecting the patient's problems, issues and concerns back to them without judgement or assumptions. They hear and understand the patient's deeper 'internal' language and how their problems are affecting them. They act as a guide to building patient self-awareness, empowering and motivating their patients to collaborate with them and develop solutions for greater conversion, engagement and outcomes.

CASE STUDY

A great example of this occurred recently, while I was shadowing a therapist. During the assessment, Gillian was chatting to a conservative seventy-year-old gentleman who was sitting with his arms crossed, giving short answers. When she asked him about the prospect of being able to play golf again, he became animated, smiled and shifted in his seat. The guard came down for one split second.

Unfortunately, Gillian missed the valuable opportunity to mine his motivations and quickly moved on, discussing more pressing clinical factors.

I later pointed out to Gillian that an expert therapist would linger in that space with open questions, probing, exploring his internal dialogue fully. They'd gain a deep understanding of how the patient's external problems (health issues) were causing deeper internal problems (feelings concerning the patient's inability to play golf).

To connect, understand, formulate and offer a truly remarkable solution, Gillian realised how vital it is that therapists understand how their patients' external health issues are affecting them internally via their thoughts, feelings and behaviours. This will help her identify the full value of her solutions in future.

Based on my twenty+ years of successfully treating patients through transformational change, I've found the single most valuable area to focus on is their emotional cues: their emotive language and drivers.

Buying emotions

If you want to truly help your patients commit to a treatment programme until they achieve their wants, aims and goals, your therapists must explore the patients' buying emotions. When your therapists have been trained to do this well, it becomes a gold mine of motivation. Your therapists will be able to explore their patients' passion and energy to fuel their journey to success.

In the consultation room, therapists need to be looking at the whole picture: the language, the behaviours the patients use to express themselves:

- How do they describe where they are?
- Have they got a compelling vision?
- Whether they're expressly saying 'I want to achieve X, Y and Z', which means their empowerment is strong

The more emotion they display, the more real the future picture is to the patient. The therapist repeats their own language, especially the emotive language, back to them so they feel heard. Then the therapist repaints the picture motivationally, taking the patient to where they want to be. Ultimately, if they can't see how the therapist's solution fits with who their future self could be, the patient will not believe enough in the solution to change their behaviour.

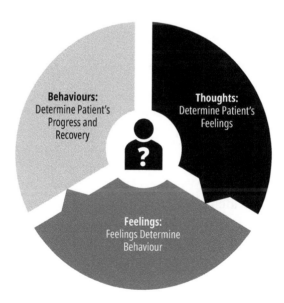

Thoughts, feelings, behaviours

Exploring their patients' buying emotions is within your therapists' scope of practice. It needs to be done in a positive, engaging way in relation to the health solutions they offer. The therapist's job is to enhance their patients' intrinsic buying motivations to encourage them to use your health services and bring about long-term transformative health change.

Patient motivations

Once your therapist has unearthed their patient's emotional cues, it's vital that they assess what the patient values: their individual motivators, aims and goals:

- Do they value low cost over high quality, or vice versa?
- Do they want to recover in time for a deadline?
- Do they want convenient appointments, eg after work or early mornings?
- Do they want a certain treatment or technique?
- What specific issues do they want solved?
- What's the highest priority for them?

Your therapist identifies these values by starting with open questions, and then drilling into specifics to discover their patient's key aims and goals. When they're discussing patient goals, it's important the therapist uses clear and defined language, making the goals specific and measurable:

THERAPIST: Regarding your recovery, what's really important or of high value to you? What's the highest priority to you?

PATIENT: I want to get better.

THERAPIST: What does getting better look like or mean to you?

Or:

PATIENT: I want to be pain free.

THERAPIST: What does pain free mean to you?

The therapist could then elaborate in the context of work, hobbies, home life aims and goals:

THERAPIST: Is that while running 10 km a week? Is that back at work, thirty-seven hours a week, fully fit?

It's important to also frame the problem in a holistic way, asking questions like:

THERAPIST: What else impacts your injury? What else does your injury impact?

Then to really illicit change, the therapist probes via change-based questions:

THERAPIST: How would you like things to be different? If you didn't have this problem, how would things be different? What would you be doing – hobbies, sports, work, activities? What are you not doing now that you'd like to be able to do?

The therapist is building a picture of their patient's motivations, gaining an understanding of their urgency:

- How badly do they want to resolve these issues?

- How quickly do they want to get better?

- How often can they attend?

- How motivated and committed are they to do what it takes to get better?

If a therapist asks open questions and practises emotive listening, they will say little but learn a lot, unearthing a goldmine of opportunity:

- How the patient's external health issue(s) are affecting them internally

- How their thoughts are affecting them emotionally

Problem solving

If your therapists implement these steps, they will discover their patients' buying motivators and identify high-value problems, so they will be able to offer specific and remarkable solutions. If they develop these skills to a high degree, they will be successful and your business will prosper. As Daniel Priestley says in his best-selling book, *24 Assets* (2017), to be successful in developing remarkable products and solutions, you first need to get a PhD in your customer's problems.

A commonly missed step in the process is discovering the high-value problems worth solving. As Daniel Pink says in his award-winning book, *To Sell Is Human* (2014), the depth or value of the problem determines the quality and worth of the solution. He concludes that in the health industry, a therapist's success depends more on the creative problem-solving skills of an artist than the reductive problem-solving skills of a technician. I agree. In my career, the most successful therapists I've worked with have been creative high-value problem identifiers.

Take for example these two problems:

- A mum with a sore elbow is unable to play tennis with her friends once a week

- A self-employed jeweller is unable to work and fulfil her orders due to her sore elbow during the busy run up to Christmas, costing her 80% of her annual revenue

Which problem is the more important to solve?

In real-life this is the same person. Through asking open questions and listening for the emotive responses, the therapist can take problem solving to the next level. Expert therapists who have developed clinical mastery tailored to a health business are constantly on the lookout for valuable problems they can solve. Essentially, the more your therapists ask open questions, listen, identify and solve high-value problems, the more successful the outcomes will be for all. Ultimately, people pay more to have big problems solved.

Armed with the valuable knowledge they've gained from their consultations, the therapist can build a remarkable solution around what their patients value and how they'll feel (internal) when the therapist has solved their problems and concerns (external). Valuable patient-therapist relationships and connections avoid all forms of awkward sales conversations.

Tangible takeaways

In this chapter, I've outlined how to transform your health businesses through connecting and building valuable patient-therapist relationships. Based on a wealth of clinical and business experience, I've shared many practical tips and techniques your therapists can implement into their clinical practice as the foundation for their patients' long-term health transformations. This is the vital second step to multiplying your profits and growing your practice with less stress and more freedom.

Here are the tangible takeaways from Step 2 of the Practice with Profit Way. Again, choose between one and two takeaways to introduce into your business per quarter, as part of your best-practice performance-management system.

1. **Patients' Charter.** As a great starting point, devise a clear Patients' Charter with input from your therapy team. It's a systemised format of what a perfect initial consultation would look like, forming the blueprint to measure and manage your therapists' performance in the consultation room. Each session can then be structured to sow the seeds of conversion into a long-term relationship until the patient achieves their aims and goals.

2. **Communication training.** Implement some team training on communication and relationship skills. Teach your therapists the costs of miscommunication to themselves, the patient and the health business in terms of confused patients, lost patients, poor outcomes and lost revenues and profits. Explain how they can

improve their communications with their patients by avoiding interruptions, providing as much affirmation as possible, summarising statements back to the patient and repeating clear, positive messages.

3. **Emotive listening.** Teach your therapists how to identify what patients value through open questions, at times drilling into the specifics to discover their key buying motivators, aims and goals. Teach therapists how to listen out for and follow emotional cues to find the patient's motivation for change using phrases like 'I'm curious, tell me more'.

4. **Problem identification.** Teach your therapists how to identify high-value problems so they can offer specific and remarkable solutions. Essentially, the more your therapist asks open questions, listens, identifies and solves high-value problems, the more successful the outcomes for your patients and the more profitable your health business will be.

By investing in your therapists and developing these inter-personal skills to mastery level, you will unlock limitless opportunities for growth and scale of your health business. By this stage of the patient journey, your therapists will have connected with their patients, discovering valuable information that forms the basis to developing remarkable solutions. They are then ready to move on to step 3 of the Practice with Profit Way, Convert.

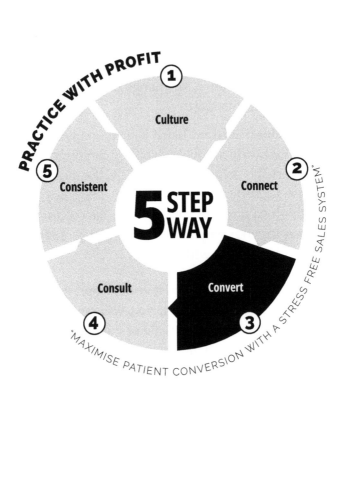

Four
Step 3 - Convert

I n this chapter, Step 3 of the Practice with Profit Way, we'll focus on how to bring the third layer of the 80/20 principle to life, transforming your health business. We'll go deeper into the consultation room and identify what it is about the top 20% of valuable patient-therapist relationships (0.8% of health-business activities) that multiplies your results.

Based on over 30,000 hours in the consultation room guiding patients to health transformations, I am confident that this step of the Practice with Profit Way leads self-funding patients into a course of treatment. Without successful patient conversions, there is no way therapists can make a lasting difference and guide patients to health transformations. This chapter will equip your therapists with best-practice professional sales skills, enabling them to convert most patients in most consultations.

Conversion conversations

The conversion conversation is at the core of a health business. It is communication with a purpose, where therapists match their service benefits with their patient's compelling reason to buy. By shifting your therapists' focus on to the number-one goal of the initial consultation – leading their ideal clients to commit to a course of treatment – you'll improve patient retention, outcomes, profits and growth.

It's interlinked with:

- **Health business's purpose:** why your business exists
- **Therapists' purpose:** why your therapists trained to help people
- **Patients' purpose:** why your patients visit your health business

The ultimate goal of the initial consultation, leading your ideal patients into a course of therapy, is why you've employed your therapists. This clarity of focus cannot be underestimated. When your therapists understand this, it can transform their careers, their patients' lives and your health business's revenues and profits.

What are you selling?

When a patient attends their initial consultation, it's important your therapists have a deep understanding of what they are buying. On the surface, they're buying a result – an outcome the therapist will deliver via therapy. But look deeper and you'll see that patients are buying the emotional benefits. How will they feel after they've used your services and returned to full health, enjoying the benefits and living the lifestyle they want? All conversion conversations should revolve around this principle with an empathetic and caring approach.

As we learned in the previous chapter, if therapists mostly use the clinical language of therapy, it's miscommunication at play. And guess what happens when the patient's pain eases and their symptoms settle – they disengage prematurely.

In any health condition, pain and symptoms are the last things to present and the first things to settle. By only focusing on the purely external health issues and symptoms, therapists leave many valuable internal or emotional lines of enquiry undiscovered, thereby limiting a patient's true potential.

Patients buy when they know you care. They aren't interested in your therapists' expertise, knowledge, credentials; they only buy your therapists' solutions when they know they care. When your therapists have taken the time to fully understand the issues from their patients' perspective, when they are authentic, motivated and believe in the solution, they'll naturally demonstrate that they care. They'll be living the behaviours that will achieve your business's vision, connecting and communicating in a profound way. Then patients will commit to your therapists and health business, long term.

Stress-free sales

After twenty plus years of training and coaching therapists, I'm used to hearing their resistance to selling various health services and solutions to patients. Not many people like to 'sell' or be 'sold' to, which is understandable, and most therapists pursue their careers because they want to help people, not sell to people. Many therapists only look at the negative connotations related to sales, like manipulation or coercion for financial gain; they haven't been trained in a stress-free sales system tailored to a health business to maximise conversions and patient transformations. This skills gap results in therapists feeling awkward and pushy when they get to the point of 'selling' their solution to their patients, performing the conversion conversation in the worst possible way. But their communication style, more than anything else, determines their patients' behaviours and outcomes.

The great news is there's no selling involved when your therapists learn to communicate how their products and services deliver health and wellbeing benefits to their patients. Instead, they communicate a genuine desire to help patients do what is in their best health interests. No manipulation, no uncomfortable feelings; just therapists who care about helping their patients achieve their aims and goals.

When your therapists believe in themselves and their therapy as the solution to their patients' health issues, it isn't selling; it's problem solving and health promotion. Then all the negative connotations and uncomfortable feelings are absent from the conversation.

I'll now describe three styles of conversion conversation, each of which will produce different patient reactions. Which style do your therapists use?

Transactional

Most therapists use a transactional style of selling. They tell the patient what they have to do, with dire consequences for patient outcomes and business success as it leaves little room for interaction.

Telling is one-sided and patients become defensive. The longer the therapists talk in a technical manner, the more the patient becomes confused. They may want to say, 'I'm not so sure, I want to think about it', but they don't have the chance.

A transactional style is the least effective conversion conversation and generally results in premature patient disengagement, which is a tough way to operate a health business.

Feature

A feature-based style is when therapists communicate purely using the technical features of their service, and is also common with therapists stuck in a clinical mindset. They're unable to clearly articulate the emotional, physical and lifestyle benefits and value of their solution in a way the patient easily understands. Patients again become confused and disengage prematurely with poor outcomes, reduced revenue and profits.

Value

The value-based approach to selling is best practice in the health industry and the most effective method for conversion conversations.

93

It starts with a connection, building a relationship and trust. This enables a climate of interaction where your therapists learn enough to understand their patients and develop the best solution to achieve their patients' unique aims and goals. It's a partnership with a superior fit, a relationship that separates your therapists from the majority of the competition.

Your therapist does not sell or push their solution. Instead, they communicate with passion and empathy, helping their patients to do what is in their best interests for a healthier life. When performed well, the value-based conversion is a natural evolution of the conversation as the patient feels confident in buying the solution.

At Practice with Profit, we teach therapists how to improve conversions through a best-practice stress-free system based around the four principles of value selling:

- **Principle 1:** identify high-value problems
- **Principle 2:** focus on the value of solving the problem
- **Principle 3:** be specific about the value you offer
- **Principle 4:** provide tangible high-value solutions

When therapists improve conversions by integrating their technical, interpersonal, problem-solving and natural sales skills into a collaborative process, they promote good health and wellbeing. They do this in a confident, positive, authentic manner with no hesitation, which takes training and practice to implement to a high degree. When they perform conversion conversations well, it takes money off the table, dramatically improves conversion rates and transforms patients' health and wellbeing. It's a win-win for all.

Identify high-value problems

A service is only valuable to the degree in which it solves a particular problem and makes a patient's life better. Finding the ideal solution to your patients' problems starts in the subjective phase of the initial consultation, outlined in Chapter Three, when your therapists identify high-value problems that their patients want solving. The more the therapists understand their patients' stories, the more likely they are to identify worthwhile problems to solve and create a service offering or treatment plan that will delight their patients. This ability to creatively identify problems sets the language, tone and trajectory of patient motivation, engagement and outcomes.

Here's a great example of two different approaches at play:

LOW-VALUE THERAPIST: You've got a bit of tennis elbow, but after a few sessions, it will settle. Don't worry, you'll be fine.

Low and behold, after two or three sessions, when the problem's starting to settle, the patient disappears. The therapist has failed to identify a high-value problem and develop a high-value solution.

In contrast, here's a therapist who has focused on identifying and solving a high-value problem for their patient:

HIGH-VALUE THERAPIST: You've developed tennis elbow. I understand your concerns – as you're a self-employed jeweller, it's costing you thousands in unfulfilled orders, and during the busy run-up to Christmas too.

I appreciate it's worsening with no sign of you being able to return to work, so let's put a plan together to get you back to work. Then we can focus on returning you to playing tennis with your friends. How does that sound?

High-value therapists take a holistic approach. They mine the patient's story for frustrations, hopes and dreams, understanding the full ramifications of their problem on their lifestyle, then use this knowledge to create remarkable services and packages that inspire their patients.

The success of your entire health business rests upon the ability of your therapists to adopt this high-value problem-identification approach.

Focus on the value of solving their problem

Before patients become interested in the solution, your therapists must help them recognise the value and benefits of solving their problems. The therapists need to understand that the patient wants a result; they're buying the emotional benefits of using the health business's products or services and how they'll feel when they've fully recovered, back to a lifestyle they enjoy.

This process is underpinned with clear, direct communication – simple messages the patients can understand. It's useful for your therapists to use the language the patient used when they were describing their issues to resonate deeply, avoid miscommunication and motivate them to move away from their pain point to recovery.

CASE STUDY

A great example of this occurred recently while I was shadowing a therapist in an audiology clinic. The audiologist was professional, charming, clinically excellent. They identified lots of interesting hearing-related problems, but didn't probe into how the patient felt. Although they performed a thorough examination and explained the diagnosis in understandable laymen's terms, they didn't relate it back to how the patient was feeling and the impacts on their day-to-day life.

When I spoke to the audiologist later, I demonstrated how focusing on the value the patient would gain when their hearing issues were solved would have led to the patient fully understanding the value of the solution. I recommended that the conversations should have gone like this:

AUDIOLOGIST: 'How does your inability to hear properly make you feel in company?'

PATIENT: 'I feel left out of the conversation, always playing catch up.'

AUDIOLOGIST: 'This hearing aid will quickly solve all the issues you're having with your hearing. You'll no longer feel left out of the conversation. You'll free up brain space, be more involved and things will be much clearer. You may even find your relationships with those close to you will improve. How does that sound?'

By understanding the full extent of the problem from their patient's perspective and presenting the emotional benefits of their solution in a natural, conversational style, this audiologist could have helped many more patients over the long term. How much more sales revenue and profit could they have generated for their health business?

A key takeaway here is that it's crucial to have your therapists well versed in adding high value to the common patient problems in your health business. Your therapists need to be flexible, adaptable and highly skilled at focusing on the value of solving the problem in laymen's terms, using the language unique to each patient.

Ramifications of inaction

An equally effective way for your therapists to highlight to your patients the value of their solution is for them to focus on the cost of not solving the problem. A prime motivation for patients is to avoid a pain point in one way or another. When the high-value solution is linked to eradicating what they want to avoid, what they don't want to see in their future selves, it is a powerful motivator.

Equip your therapists with the skills to save patients from themselves – from making ill-informed decisions, prematurely dropping-out, poor outcomes, long-term suffering and disability. Your therapists need to be adept at outlining an urgent need, including the full ramifications of not solving their patients' health problems. Without this urgency, their chances of leading their patients to successful health transformations are slim.

There is a time and a place to challenge patients with tough love, using language that may be perceived as negative, but communicating it in a motivational manner is critical to patient success. This is a major blind spot for therapists who suffer with the mistaken belief that their patients are already sold on the solution; otherwise why would they have booked the consultation in the first place?

Ultimately, your patients are paying for your therapists' expert opinion, so your therapists need to give it professionally and unemotionally. It's then up to the patient what they decide to do with it.

The reality is there are real and avoidable consequences of your patients not following the therapists' recommendations. These are not scare tactics; your therapists have identified all the information in the patients' unique stories, explored their thoughts and feelings, how their problems have affected them to date and what they want to avoid. Your therapists are acting like a mirror, reflecting back the patients' problems in a way that resonates, using language that patients understand to connect and drive positive change. This process draws their patients' attention to potential pitfalls they may not have recognised, helping them make better-informed decisions, improving conversion and successful outcomes.

For best results, your therapists should use both these approaches:

- Explain the ramifications of doing nothing
- Focus on the positive value to be gained by solving their patients' problems, moving their patients towards the benefits and solutions

At this stage, the expert therapist listens to see which of the two messages resonates more with the patient. Then they prioritise that clear and simple message throughout the patient journey to materialise long-term health transformations.

Be specific about the value you offer

In a health business, the commercial journey and the patient journey are entwined. There is clearly an immediate financial cost to the patient, so to be successful, your therapists need get specific about the value they offer to each patient. They achieve this by clearly matching their patient's wants with service benefits while packaging their needs.

- **Wants:** what a patient wants, or their buying motivator, is the reason they have booked an appointment. An example could be to solve their knee problem, return to running and lose weight for an important wedding.

- **Benefits:** these include the emotional benefits of how they'll feel after they've purchased and used your products and services. In this example, the benefits are losing weight to feel confident and look great in their wedding photos.

- **Needs:** these are the treatments the therapist needs to perform to enable the patient to achieve their aims and goals. In this case, it's the individual treatments to get the patient back running.

It sounds simple enough, the only issue being therapists rarely discuss the emotional benefits of the health business's products and services, which are the most powerful motivators for transformative change. Instead they focus purely on the needs, discussing the technical features in detail which is where they're most comfortable, but this can confuse their patients and drastically reduce conversion.

By teaching your therapists how to successfully match the patient's wants with the solution's benefits while packaging the patient's needs, you'll ensure they'll become masters of the conversion conversation. It's much simpler to understand when we see it in action.

THERAPIST: I understand you want to solve your knee problem to get back to running so you can lose weight and look and feel great for your big day.

PATIENT: Yeah, that would be great, thanks.

THERAPIST: Well don't worry, you're in the right place. If you follow my treatment plan, we'll get you back to doing short jogs in two to three weeks. You'll feel much more confident as you start to get fitter, then we'll progress you to longer jogs within four weeks. By then you'll be back on track, losing weight and feeling much fitter for the wedding day. How does that sound?

PATIENT: Great, let's do it.

While treating the patient, the therapist can describe the treatment benefits in more detail, explaining how each one will lead the patient to achieving their wants, aims and goals.

Even at this stage, it's important the patient doesn't get bogged down in technical details of the features or treatment techniques. Keep the messages in laymen's terms, positive and focused on the emotional benefits.

Knowledge and expertise

When it comes to value, the therapist's job is to convince their patient of their solution's value; that it's worth investing in a remarkable packaged solution of products and services to achieve the patient's aims and goals. To do this effectively, knowledge is power.

The more your therapists know about their patient, the better they can explain the benefits they offer. Your therapists need to be skilful at selecting and highlighting the small subset of their service offerings that are most relevant to addressing each patient's problems and concerns. This is what they've trained to do, but often they confuse their patients by focusing on the technical, clinical features, not the value.

For example:

FEATURE-FOCUSED THERAPIST: Your biceps femoris
has a grade 2 tear, so we need to first resolve the
inflammation. We'll start with some specific soft tissue
mobilisations, possibly some deep transverse frictions,
and then apply some Kinesio tape for a few sessions.
As you improve, we'll increase the load capacity
through a series of progressive resistance training. How
does that sound?

PATIENT: Err...

STEP 3 - CONVERT

There is a communication gap here. To the therapist, the solution they're offering is simple; to a patient, it's highly confusing. The therapist needs to understand this gap, simplify their language while matching the service benefits with the patient's wants, values and buying motives.

With a value-focused therapist, the conversation would go like this:

VALUE-FOCUSED THERAPIST: You have a medium-grade tear to one of your hamstring muscles. It's sore and painful at present, but don't worry. If you follow the treatment programme I recommend, you'll be back running up to five miles pain free within the next four weeks maximum. We'll start with some massage, and then tape it to help improve the healing. It will give you comfort, support and pain-relief as you move about in between sessions. Then we'll start with some light strengthening exercises, progressing them as you improve. How does that sound?

PATIENT: Sounds great, let's make a start.

It really doesn't have to be complicated. Communicating with patients in laymen's terms to paint a positive picture of a successful future, using a message that resonates with them, that they understand easily, your therapists will motivate them to use your health business's products and services to achieve their aims and goals.

Assumptions

Both therapists and patients come into the consultation room heavily loaded with a wide range of assumptions. Unaddressed assumptions reduce the value of the solution and limit conversion, which are big issues for a health business. They act as barriers to patient recovery, limiting revenue, profit, growth and success.

Assumptions are based on a wide variety of myths:

- There's a free National Health Service (NHS) alternative
- An evidence-based focus is best
- A technical communication style is best
- The solution isn't worth the money
- Problem identification and solving aren't necessary
- The solution won't fit with the patient's diary and schedule

Examining these assumptions is beyond the scope of this book, but it is fully addressed in the Practice with Profit Health Business Accelerator programme. To give you some insight, though, I'll tackle one major assumption.

Value, not price

Many people in the health industry are uncomfortable with making profit from someone else's pain. These hang-ups often result in therapists undermining their patients' recovery process with their verbal and non-verbal communication when they're outlining a solution. They're hesitant and stumble when they mention price, and their patients can sense their reluctance.

Therapists really need to learn the whole story from the patient's perspective, understanding what their patient has invested in their journey to date to identify the full value of the solution. Consider a simple example of a podiatrist who is treating a runner whose marathon training programme has been cut short by injury. The podiatrist may not see the value in the £400 treatment because they don't have the £1,000 worth of sponsorship the marathon runner has. They also haven't pre-booked a weekend trip away with friends to run the marathon, not forgetting the sore muscles and achy legs the runner has endured so far.

Therapists working in any health business need the skills to educate their patients on value. To be successful and build a thriving health business, your therapists should focus on value, not price.

Self-worth

Invest in your therapists to develop their self-belief so they can deliver great value and outcomes to their patients.

To improve a therapist's self-worth, it's helpful to focus them on:

- How many years did they spend on gaining their qualifications?

- How much did it cost them to qualify, including tuition fees, student loans, the cost of living at university?

- How many hours did they spend learning their craft and skills on a minimum wage?

- How many weekends have they spent on training courses?

Once your therapists start adding these up, they'll often realise that they are under-selling their value and worth.

Therapists need to see the value in themselves, and the products and services they deliver. Ultimately, if your therapists don't support the pricing and profit structure of your health business, if they don't believe they are worth it, you need to educate them, otherwise they're a liability.

Objections

When it comes to selling themselves and their treatment solutions, your therapists shouldn't be afraid of resistance or push-back. With a stress-free sales system, it doesn't happen often, which demonstrates when your therapists are consistently providing full and remarkable solutions.

When resistance does occur, they'll need to know how to deal with it simply and professionally to ensure all barriers to recovery are removed. Therapists can respond to objections using these three steps:

- **Sympathise:** identify with the patient's concerns and objections

- **Explanation:** choose benefits that justify the solution

- **Clarification:** ask directly if they've satisfied the objection or concern

It's crucial your therapists believe in what they are providing as the best-fit solution. You need motivated therapists in touch with their why, passionate about what they do.

Here's an example of how to deal with patient resistance:

PATIENT PRICE OBJECTION: Can I leave it until pay day in a couple of weeks as it's been an expensive month?

THERAPIST SYMPATHY: I can understand your financial concerns. It seems like a lot of money, but as you pointed out earlier, what's the cost of not being able to walk? You're hobbling about in pain, putting on weight, feeling lousy, stuck at home, unable to go out, bored.

THERAPIST EXPLANATION: If we reduce the frequency of treatment prematurely, at best your progress and benefits will plateau. You'll be prolonging your problem, and you've already been suffering for two months. At worst, you'll do something silly over the next week, make it worse and relapse, then you'll be at risk of having to start over again. You'll be demoralised. I don't want that to happen to you, you're doing so well. You're in a good place now, so by continuing further treatment and not delaying, you will improve things further, and in a week or so, we'll reduce the frequency of treatment and you'll be back on full duties at work, feeling much better.

THERAPIST CLARIFICATION: How does that sound? What do you say?

Always link the benefits to the patient's buying motivators to add value. Your therapists and services are not a commodity and the patients are not choosing you based on price.

Provide tangible high-value solutions

Your ideal self-funding patients are busy people. They don't appreciate being involved in consultations or conversations that leave them wondering why they just wasted their valuable time.

The fourth principle in leading patients into a successful course of treatment is to start providing value in the initial consultation. This is a key concept if you want to transform your health business and build a profitable practice. For this to occur, the value your therapists provide needs to be far in excess of what your patients may expect for the price they are paying.

This is when your therapists put all their clinical knowledge and skills to the test, providing treatment and giving quick benefits to the patient. It's crucial they go for the easy, quick wins that provide the most tangible benefits to demonstrate their expertise and value, improving conversion. In the first session, it's paramount that the therapist gives the patients at least a fifteen-minute sample of the quality of treatment they can expect during their journey to recovery.

Imagine a patient with a grade 2 calf strain. They're limping, experiencing a sharp stab as they walk. By simply adding a heel wedge, the therapist can immediately decrease their pain and improve mobility, and they'll be impressed. That's what they're paying your therapists for: immediate dramatic results. I've met lots of therapists in similar circumstances who wouldn't think to get a heel wedge from the stock room, but their lethargy in the initial consultation means that patients are more likely to be hesitant to engage.

The initial appointment and gaining the conversion, bringing it all together to wow the patient, is one of my favourite parts of being a therapist. Make sure your therapists give immediate benefit, a direct focus on solving their patients' problems, demonstrating that they're the expert to guide them to recovery. They're the one to trust.

In the consultation room, as in all walks of life, your therapists will reap what they sow. This is what your therapists have trained to do, this is their time to shine. A health business will only get paid for what its therapists do, what value they add and ultimately the results they achieve, so in the consultation room, actions truly speak louder than words. Actions get the conversion, which is the ultimate goal of the first session. If patients don't return, your therapists will never get a chance to help them towards health transformations.

Time management

Your therapists must be natural, authentic and passionate about helping patients achieve their aims and goals. They should have a focus on adding value with treatment, advice, exercises, product demos, exercise demos, showing their patients video clips, escorting them around the practice, educating them on how your health business is different. You want the patient to have the confidence to back your therapists to make a difference to their lives, and it's crucial that they find this confidence in the first session, so no time management excuses.

If the therapist is running out of time, they can cut their subjective or objective assessment short, but they must not cut the valuable therapy section short or the next consultation may never happen. If your therapists fail to provide adequate value, your service will be intangible to the patients and you'll be asking them to take a risk on a promise to get better. And we all know what most patients do when things get risky: they disappear. Who can blame them?

I cannot remember the amount of times I've seen therapists get bogged down in the assessments while offering no treatment at all in the first consultation. They've ticked all the clinical boxes in their head, oblivious to the patient's decision-making and buying habits, with a cheap promise that 'We'll start treatment next session'. The patients then often choose to vote with their feet, never to return.

Personal recovery plan

During the initial consultation, it's also vital your therapists discuss the realistic expectation for the coming weeks, linking it to the frequency of treatment, tailored to the patient's unique aims and goals. This builds crucial patient momentum for successful outcomes.

A great way to summarise this conversation at the end of the initial consultation is to give every patient a bespoke personal recovery plan (PRP) to take away. It adds value while improving the tangibility of your service and patient conversion. In the PRP, it's vital to emphasise the benefits the patient will get from your therapy, so keep your choice of words focused on what the customer gets, not what you give.

Personal Recovery Plan
gophysio

For	
Therapist	
Date	

Diagnosis

(Your initial diagnosis is based on a snapshot in time & may be altered or modified slightly as your treatment progresses).

Personal Advice & Recommendations

Services or products you'd benefit from that we offer at goPhysio:

Sports Massage	Massage Wax	Ice Pack	Yoga
Pilates Classes	Gym Ball	Heat Pack	Rehabilitation
Resistive Exercise Band	Orthopaedic Pillow	Chiropody	
Foot Insoles / Orthotics	Taping	Back Rack	
Massager Brace / Support	Massage Roller / Ball		
Other:			

If you need to contact your physiotherapist, you can email them directly at their personal email, which is their first name @gohysiotherapy.co.uk

Any appointment enquiries can be made by calling 023 8025 3317 or emailing mail@gohysiotherapy.co.uk. You can also book appointments online by visiting our website www.gohysiotherapy.co.uk

Example of a personal recovery plan

A PRP may consist of this information:

- Patient wants, aims and goals
- Diagnosis and prognosis, if they follow the recommendations
- Agreed treatment plan with benefits
- Timeline and appointment frequency
- Recommended products and other services
- Contact details, showing you care
- Therapist and patient signatures to seal the deal.

I recommend you present the PRP to the patient with your glossy health-business brochure detailing your full ecosystem of services.

The successful close

When your therapists perform conversion conversations well, it negates the need to ask for the sale, which will not be an abrupt surprise or stressful, pressurised event at the end of the initial consultation, but a natural evolution of conversation. For example:

THERAPIST: Right, let's go down and book those appointments. Continuing later this week, we'll do a lot more treatment and you'll feel the benefits immediately. You'll feel looser, more mobile, in less pain etc. We'll then progress you further and get you closer towards achieving those aims and goals.

Your therapists will then have achieved the ultimate aim of the initial consultation: converting their patients into customers for your health business.

Tangible takeaways

In this chapter, we've looked at how to transform your health business through focusing on the main aim of the initial consultation: leading high-value self-funding patients into a course of treatment. In other words, converting those patients into health-business customers. I've included many practical tips and techniques your therapists can implement into their clinical practice, guiding their patients on their journey from pain to gain, achieving their wants, aims and goals. This is the vital third step to multiplying your profits and growing your practice with less stress and more freedom.

Here are eight tangible takeaways to teach your therapists how to become masters of the conversion conversation. Choose between one and two takeaways to introduce into your business per quarter as part of your best-practice performance management system.

1. **Conversion conversations.** Starting today, teach your therapists that the ultimate goal of the initial consultation is to lead your ideal patients into a course of therapy to achieve their wants and goals. Explain this conversion goal in positive terms, relevant to its impact on their career, patient success and outcomes, and health-business revenues and profit.

2. **What are they selling?** Give your therapists a deep understanding of what they're selling and what

their patients are buying: the emotional benefits of how they'll feel after they've used your services and returned to full health.

3. **Stress-free sales.** Help your therapists experience a mindset shift from being uncomfortable and afraid of professional sales to having great sales skills. Do a stress-free sales presentation with material from this book, asking them what their current opinions are around sales, and teach them there's no 'selling' when they communicate how your products and services deliver health and wellbeing benefits to their patients. Instead, there's a genuine desire and motivation to help patients do what is in their best health interests to achieve their aims and goals.

4. **Identify high-value problems.** Teach your therapists practically that the more they understand their patient's story, the more likely they are to identify high-value problems that are worthwhile for their patients to solve.

5. **Focus on the value of solving their patient's problem.** To improve the value of their solution, your therapists should help their patients move away from pain, outlining the consequences of inaction, while moving their patients towards recovery and the positive value to be gained by solving their problem.

6. **Be specific about the value on offer.** Teach your therapists how to be specific about the value their solution offers by matching the service benefits with their patients' buying motives, focusing on the emotional benefits.

7. **Provide value.** Teach your therapists how to provide maximum value with quick wins in the initial consultation. They need to understand that to gain a successful conversion, from their patient's point of view, the value they provide must exceed the price of the consultation.

8. **Tangibility.** Improve the tangibility of your service offering and gain greater conversion by giving each patient a PRP at the end of their initial consultation.

At this stage of their journey, the patient has completed their initial consultation, agreeing to a course of treatment with follow-up bookings. They are now moving into the next stage of their recovery journey, the follow-up consultations, which are covered in the next chapter, step 4 of the Practice with Profit Way.

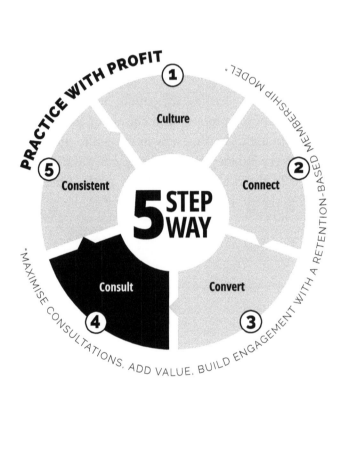

PRACTICE WITH PROFIT

1 Culture

2 Connect

3 Convert

4 Consult

5 Consistent

5 STEP WAY

"BUILD A RETENTION-BASED MEMBERSHIP MODEL."

"MAXIMISE CONSULTATIONS, ADD VALUE, BUILD ENGAGEMENT WITH A RETENTION-BASED MEMBERSHIP MODEL."

Five
Step 4 – Consult

In this chapter, I'll take you deep into the fourth layer of the 80/20 principle and highlight the many opportunities for growth and scale that currently exist in the consultation rooms of your health business. We'll examine Step 4 of the Practice with Profit Way: Consult, specifically follow-up consultations, which are a crucial part of this retention-based formula to health-business growth.

Following the successful patient journey through each consultation, I'll show you the tips and techniques clinical masters use to optimise patients' recovery until they achieve their aims and goals, providing true health transformations while multiplying the health business's revenues, profit and growth. We'll explore practical ways your therapists can continually add value in regular consultations throughout the whole patient journey.

When your therapists are taking great care of their patients, the patients will take great long-term care of your business.

Trust

Trust is the foundation on which all long-term relationships rest. It is built on tangible evidence that your therapists will do what they promise.

When patients rely on your therapists to deliver on promises, they are putting their valuable resources – health, time, money and outcomes – in a vulnerable position. In many cases, should the therapist fail to perform, the impact on the patient's commitments – work, family and health – could be extreme.

Most people fear the unknown, so they carry scepticism and suspicion into their relationships as a means of protecting themselves from vulnerability. On the whole, patients will do everything possible to minimise risk, often putting up with their health issues rather than risking buying therapy from your health business. To build the essential trust with their patients, your therapists need to be sincere and believe in what they are selling.

When conversion, engagement and attendance are poor in a health business, it's often a stark indication that patient-therapist trust is an issue. To put this into context, your health business's biggest threat is not the practice down the road; it is a lack of patient trust. This is symptomised by a lack of understanding and poor decision making, leading to patients failing to attend their follow-up consultations.

An important aspect of building trust is being able to help the patient put the consequences of doing nothing, failing to convert, early self-discharge, into context, and the costly impact this would have on their recovery. Trust in business relationships means providing consistent evidence that you keep your promises.

Building trust can be likened to making deposits in an emotional bank account. As your therapists make deposits through keeping their commitments and delivering on their promises, the balance of trust in the account grows. If they fail to honour their commitments, break their promises, behave in an unlikeable or inconsistent way, make the patient feel unimportant or unappreciated, they make withdrawals from their trust account.

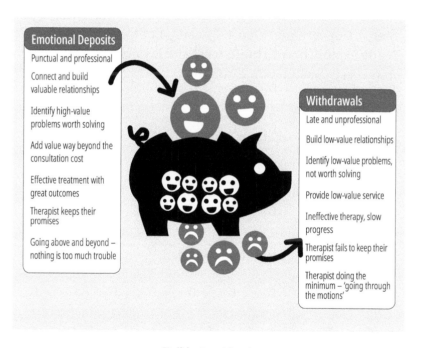

Emotional Deposits
Punctual and professional

Connect and build valuable relationships

Identify high-value problems worth solving

Add value way beyond the consultation cost

Effective treatment with great outcomes

Therapist keeps their promises

Going above and beyond – nothing is too much trouble

Withdrawals
Late and unprofessional

Build low-value relationships

Identify low-value problems, not worth solving

Provide low-value service

Ineffective therapy, slow progress

Therapist fails to keep their promises

Therapist doing the minimum – 'going through the motions'

Build a trust bank

The figure above illustrates common ways your therapists can make deposits or withdrawals from their trust accounts.

If your therapists make too many withdrawals, they'll lose trust and their patients will go elsewhere. If they make enough deposits, they'll build trust and the patients will successfully convert into long-term customers for your health business. A large percentage of those will become loyal brand advocates and sign up for recurring income-generating membership services. Either way, though, your patients will choose with their feet and their wallets. They'll either stay and pay, or walk away. There is no clearer feedback.

Teach your therapists that trust is something they build in each and every consultation. It starts with Step 2 of the Practice with Profit Way, Connect, and continues through Step 3, Convert, into Step 4, Consult. But this is where we'll really explore how to build trust and loyalty, strengthening it in every consultation through:

- Adding value
- Frequent consultations
- Caring conversations
- Goal setting and gamification
- Nudge theory

Let's look at each point in more detail.

Adding value

Building patient-therapist relationships and adding value through the recovery journey are fundamental principles to transforming your health business for profit, growth and scale. They are without doubt the best ways to cement a patient's commitment to the recovery plan.

To add value to a high degree, your therapists have to ensure the value the patient experiences in each consultation exceeds the price they pay. It's the emotional bank account in action. This is ultimately where business skills merge with clinical skills in the consultation room. It is the true measure of clinical mastery tailored to a health business.

As health-business leaders, we need to remember that therapists are intelligent people, but with a purely clinical focus, they'll be stuck in the rut of making excuses, telling stories. They'll spin things with academia rather than practical change. In a private health business, this approach doesn't work. We're measured by market forces and cannot bank academia, low productivity or poor performance. In a health business, all we can bank is what a patient has spent in our business, which is a direct measurement of how much value our therapists are creating and delivering in the consultation room.

If your health business's revenues are low, if you feel you're not getting adequately rewarded, the reason is simple: your therapists are not adding enough value in the consultation room. What your health business banks is a true reflection of the value your therapists are adding to your patients' lives. It's pure behavioural economics: the more time and money your patients are prepared to spend with their therapist, solving their injury problems and concerns, the more value they're experiencing. If patients think your therapists are worth it, they'll attend regularly and happily pay for it. The more engaged and committed the patient, the better the outcomes and the more likely they are to achieve their aims and goals.

As this area of clinical expertise is a particular favourite of mine, I've identified numerous ways your therapists can add value in the consultation room throughout their patient's journey, closely linked to all elements of your health business strategy and positioning. It starts with your therapists combining their interpersonal (communication and relationship) skills with stress-free sales skills to boost performance and improve quality of care. Then during the follow-up consultations, your therapists can add value through:

- **Consultation structure:** prioritising therapy, providing tangible benefit above all else

- **Multi-modal consultations:** using a variety of different treatment techniques per consultation

- **Initial quick wins:** relieving symptoms quickly

- **Bespoke advice:** self-treatment advice to maintain benefits and build momentum

- **Treatment aids:** convenient product demos and sales

- **PRPs:** to improve service tangibility

- **Digital software solutions:** emailed advice, exercises and appointment reminders

- **Chaperoning:** therapist chaperones the patient to reception with formal handover

- **Follow-ups:** frequent follow-up consultations to build momentum

Without a formalised training approach that's aligned with the skills and techniques of the previous three steps of the Practice with Profit Way, most therapists fail to add adequate value. Instead, they often expect to get rewarded for what they know, as opposed to what they do in the consultation room. This is a major issue for healthcare businesses – it's why patients disengage prematurely. From a customer viewpoint, the benefits aren't worth the risks and they vote with their wallet and feet.

Adding value in the consultation room results in patient commitment and engagement in the form of regular attendance, which builds momentum and success. The overall aim is to differentiate your health business through added value at every touchpoint to transform it and be able to sell at premium prices, enjoying high margins by delivering exceptional service to a large segment of self-funding customers.

Frequent consultations

If your patients are not spending time in frequent consultations with your therapists, it's a sign your therapists are just solving small problems, adding little value. They've become enablers of poor outcomes, with patient suffering, chronicity and disability the result.

Ultimately, your therapists cannot help patients experience great outcomes, guiding them to health transformations, without spending regular quality one-to-one time with them in the consultation room. This is without doubt the single most important factor in your health business's success.

Therapists spending time with patients in frequent, regular consultations has these benefits:

- It builds valuable patient-therapist relationships
- It builds engagement and momentum

- It trains patients in how to recover

- It develops therapists' clinical mastery

In my twenty+ years as a therapist, I've never helped a patient in a meaningful, valuable or lasting way who didn't commit to the treatment plan, attend regular appointments and spend time with me in face-to-face consultations. Without frequent consultations, it just can't be done. Whatever specialism of healthcare your business is in, it's all about people and behavioural change.

Caring conversations

Caring conversations need to occur in every consultation, guiding the patient on their recovery journey. Ultimately, your therapists became therapists to help people. To be excellent at solving patients' problems, building motivation for change, they need to be able to press the sore spot for personal growth.

One of the reasons caring and potentially emotional conversations are so powerful when it comes to patient commitment to a course of therapy and behavioural change is because people buy emotionally and back their decision up logically. If your therapists focus on telling their patients about the technical features of treatment, the patients will focus on price and your service will become a commodity in their eyes. By equipping your therapists with the skills to discuss the emotional benefits, like how the patient will feel when they're better, you'll ensure they engage with the emotional part of the patient's brain, and then price becomes irrelevant.

When your therapists frame their solutions from this perspective, for a brief moment, the patient has already recovered in their mind's eye. They're imagining themselves in the future after they've successfully used your products and services to achieve their aims and goals, and they want it.

This is essentially neurolinguistic programming (NLP), which is a highly useful technique for therapists to use throughout the initial and follow-up consultations to build trust, momentum, engagement and commitment to behavioural change with the patients, all of which they'll require to achieve their aims and goals. Obviously, it needs to be backed up with tangible evidence, therapy and continued wins.

With all this energy invested in emotive conversations, providing value with a patient-centred focus, your therapists must remain professional and create boundaries within their clinical practices. While giving best-practice treatment recommendations based on your health business's care pathways and their clinical expertise, they also need to establish clear consequences for patients who don't follow their advice.

Some patients will attempt to water down the treatment plan, take short cuts, shave off some consultations to save time and money. If your therapists comply, it often renders the treatment plan ineffective.

This tends to happen when your therapists haven't identified a valuable problem worth solving. If their solution doesn't offer a distinctively higher value than any of the other options the patient is considering, they need to do something about it or qualify out. If they let their patients modify their recovery plan, they become enablers of poor outcomes and chronicity.

The patient will ultimately blame them for the poor outcomes, complain and want a refund. They may even badmouth your health business and leave one-star reviews for all of eternity.

Going forward, it's crucial your therapists are not too flexible with their recommendations and expertise. Clinical experts don't play that game, and your therapists can avoid it by finding a valuable problem worth solving, with the associated high levels of patient motivation and engagement. Ultimately, who is the expert: the therapist or the patient?

Here's an example of a therapist clearly discussing their recommendations and the consequences of the patient not following them:

THERAPIST: OK, John, based on my findings, I'm recommending I see you a further two times this week, twice next week and once every four to five days thereafter until we have you back to running fitness, ready for the race in four weeks' time. That's a total of seven to nine sessions over the next four weeks. How does that sound?

PATIENT: That's a lot of sessions. The problem is I'm busy all this week and could only make one session next week. Would that work?

THERAPIST: I'm sorry to hear that, but if we now leave it ten days before your next session, and then meet once a week, that's only three to four sessions before your race. It's not possible, you won't make it. The longer you leave it between sessions, the slower you'll improve, and you'll run out of time.

PATIENT: Oh, right.

THERAPIST: You're paying for my expertise and time today, and ultimately an outcome. Based on what you've told me, you can't wait to get back to running so you can complete that event in four weeks' time. Is that correct?

PATIENT: Yes.

THERAPIST: The bottom line is I want to get you better as quickly as possible, but you have to attend twice this week, twice next week, then every four to five days. How much do you want to do that race?

PATIENT: Quite badly. It's my thirtieth birthday and I want to do a personal best.

THERAPIST: Well, those two sessions twice weekly will give benefit, easing spasms and pain, improving healing. You'll feel more mobile, then as I continue to see you, you'll get better quickly. I'll have you back to light jogging within two weeks if you commit to this programme, then I'll progress you from there to getting back to running for that race in four weeks. How does that sound?

PATIENT: Yeah, let's do it!

I encourage therapists to set boundaries with their patients to maintain momentum. Clear boundaries, challenging the patient while following best-practice principles in motivation and behavioural change science, educate the patients to make the correct decisions for their welfare and recovery. Train them to recovery, save them from themselves.

Goal setting and gamification

When patients have bought into why they're visiting your health business, they're much more likely to achieve their goals, but to do that, they need to know exactly what their goals are. Goal setting is therefore a valuable part of the trust-building process.

Goal setting should bring all the individual elements together: the patient's high-value problems, their wants and aims, and the emotional benefits of achieving them. In collaboration with your therapists, patients need to develop one specific, measurable, achievable, realistic and time-bound (SMART) goal, aligned to their image of themselves in the future, fully recovered. The goal must be transformative.

Your therapists can then help their patients break down the main SMART goal into achievable mini-goals, or hurdles as I like to call them, along their road to recovery. As the patients progress through the various stages of treatment and jump the hurdles, your therapists map their achievements, improving motivation and engagement.

For example, in the world of musculoskeletal medicine, the road to recovery can be defined in three phases, each with its own unique hurdles to jump to progress into the next stage:

1. **Pain dominant.** In this phase, your therapists talk about easing pain, improving the patient's range of motion, reducing swelling, improving mobility. They refer to the positive benefits of feeling looser, moving more freely with less stiffness and tightness, reinforcing the correct behaviour and progress through objective and

subjective signs. With an injured runner, this could mean the therapist deactivating the myofascial trigger points while improving the patient's calf flexibility and ankle range of motion.

2. **Load dominant.** In this phase, the mini-goals or hurdles are more strength or load based and can also relate to function. Again, the therapist references the benefits of feeling stronger, more confident, more able, linking this to objective and subjective markers. In our runner, the hurdles could be pain-free hopping, jogging on the spot or shuttle runs. The therapist has helped them break down their end goal and devise specific hurdles. In other words, they've gamified the process to maintain patient motivation and commitment.

3. **Goal dominant.** In this phase, the patient's hurdles are goal specific. In our injured runner example, the therapist introduces a return to running programme, which could be in the form of a run-walk programme with specific progressions relative to the patient's recovery levels, aims and goals.

With defined hurdles to clear as they return to full function, the patient is motivated. In each consultation, they're keen to tell their therapist of their successes, because the therapist has positively reinforced the behavioural change and achievement of outcomes by outlining the benefits the patient will feel, the momentum they'll build and their progress. The patient experiences regular boosts in mood and motivation as they work along their road to recovery under professional guidance with collaboration and positive reinforcement.

This is gamification. It's a holistic approach to patient management, a great way to revise and progress goals, as they can be ever-changing and need to evolve in line with patient progress, improving motivation within the patient's recovery programme.

Nudge theory

Another principle used widely in healthcare to improve commitment to behavioural change and the achievement of health goals is nudge theory. It works by therapists gently nudging patients in the direction they'd like them to move, encouraging patients to make wise decisions for their welfare and achieve great health and wellbeing outcomes. The approach gives the patients the impression that they have a choice between two paths, while the therapist is using small targeted nudges to send them the right way to achieve their goals.

Here are a few examples of small targeted nudges your therapists could implement in your practice today to encourage positive behavioural change, engagement and improved patient outcomes:

THERAPIST: As we discussed, Pilates is an excellent way for you to actively maintain the benefits. You won't be reliant on me for episodic treatment; you'll be in control. So, which would suit you better, mat-based Pilates or reformer Pilates?

Or:

THERAPIST: You're doing well, so to keep you progressing, you'll need to see me for two consultations next week.

Which days suit you better, Monday and Thursday, or Tuesday and Friday?

Or:

THERAPIST: As we've discussed, orthotics are crucial to your recovery. Which would you prefer, one pair at £350 or two pairs for £549?

Or:

THERAPIST: You're now in the load-dominant phase, so I can refer you into the rehabilitation class or we can do one-to-one sessions in the strong room with weights. Which would suit you better?

I'm sure you get the picture.

Your therapists need to be adopting nudge theory with every one of their patients in every consultation. Ultimately, it's not a case of 'if'; it's a case of 'when'. Here are the two options, the patient decides which would suit them better. It's active action-orientated language, optimising outcomes and protecting patients from themselves; a clear and simple but highly effective way to nudge patients in the correct direction for transformational change. I suggest you teach your therapists to use it now.

Loyalty

If you want to have a profitable practice, retain and gain more A-star self-funding patients and keep your career upwardly mobile, your therapists must strive in every consultation to leave their patients wanting more.

Imagine if your health business's patients:

- Really looked forward to their treatment
- Would never consider seeing any competitors
- Were forgiving of any shortfalls and service issues

The aim is for your therapists to become their patients' trusted health advisors within their specialism. When your therapist's patient rings up and says, '*I didn't even bother to ring the GP for this problem, I thought I'd just come straight and see your therapist instead. They're the expert*', you know your therapist is well on the way to building pre-eminence and clinical mastery tailored to your health business.

By following the five-step Practice with Profit Way, your therapists build loyalty, which is essential to retaining and gaining ideal clients:

- Loyal patients make great decisions for their welfare, following your therapists' recommendations every time
- Loyal patients don't push back, so there are no awkward sales conversations, only stress-free sales
- Loyal patients vote with their feet and wallet, choosing to visit and spend money in your health business regularly
- Loyal patients have low cancellation rates, and all cancellations are genuine and appointments urgently rescheduled
- Loyal patients sign up for long-term membership and subscription services

- Loyal patients become brand advocates, recommending your business to their family and friends

- Loyalty beats the competition every time

- Loyalty does a lot of the marketing work for you and your team

Loyalty is the reward your patients will give your business in return for your therapists following the Practice with Profit Way and taking care of them. A one-consultation wonder is a one-off event; loyalty is ongoing. Your business will gain loyalty over the long term as positive patient experiences add up and your patients trust that you really care about them.

Memberships

A great way to add to the emotional trust bank, building and rewarding loyalty, is to offer your most frequent ideal clients a membership option. Membership is a recurring income-generating business model, which is one of the most successful business models over the last 500 hundred years. John Warrillow in his excellent book, *The Automatic Customer* (2015), gives an overview of the history of the subscription or membership business model, from early map publishers in the 1500s to newspapers and magazines of the 1700s to Amazon Prime.

Before we look at proceeding down this highly rewarding route in your health business, here's a little detour around membership model education. New membership businesses are often referred to as a 'J' curve business model as they typically:

- Involve a significant amount of upfront investment

- Are unprofitable for the first few years, signified by a dip in the J curve

- Push through this unprofitable period, if they're successful, often experiencing a prolonged period of growth signified by vertical line in the J

The great news is the high risk associated with a 'J' curve membership model can be removed in any established health business that has already built a database of satisfied customers. Instead of paying each time for a service, clients pay a set monthly fee and get access to options based on their level of membership. Think of it like a Netflix membership with health benefits.

Currently, in the health and wellbeing space, gyms are leading the membership model race. Over the last ten years, the lines between healthcare and gyms have blurred, and I don't see this changing any time soon. This is a good thing as in the last twelve months, we've started to see recurring income-generating membership models becoming the next big thing in the health and wellness industry.

There is rapid growth in bespoke health and wellbeing memberships, whether it's for Pilates, massage, acupuncture, dental practices or beauty salons and everything in between. Instead of looking at these services as a once-in-a-while luxury, customers (or patients) view them as regular necessities. Maintaining a healthy body or healthy smile is a commitment that once people start, they have to maintain. This maintenance can add up, which is one reason why health businesses are offering subscription models to their frequent customers.

A few years ago, my health business modified its block-booking Pilates programme into a membership-only service. This moved it from a transactional health and wellbeing service to a recurring income-generating model. It took at least six months of planning and preparation, but it was worth it. It reduced the inevitable eight course churn, improving retention and growth, and the business is in the process of expanding this model to include other services. This is a reality for my business and it can be a reality for you and your health business too. It just takes a growth mindset and a guide with the practical strategy and know-how to implement successfully.

Tangible takeaways

In this chapter, we've covered Step 4 of the Practice with Profit Way, Consult, bringing the fourth layer of the 80/20 principle to life. We've learned how to improve patient engagement and retention through added value in each and every consultation until patients achieve their aims and goals. We've explored the principles and practical approaches to equip your therapists with the knowledge and skills to take better care of their patients throughout the whole journey from pain to gain.

Implementing this step into your health business will ensure your patients become loyal brand advocates, and a large percentage will convert into long-term customers and advocates. Here are seven tangible takeaways to implement into your health business to multiply your profits and grow your practice with less stress and more freedom. Choose between one and two takeaways to introduce into your business per quarter as part of your best-practice performance-management system.

1. **Trust.** Teach your therapists that trust is something they build in their emotional bank account in every consultation. Train them in the techniques to build trust and loyalty consistently with each patient.

2. **Adding value.** Teach your therapists how to add value in every consultation. To do this, they can structure the consultation to prioritise treatments that provide quick wins and symptom relief, including convenient product demos and sales to speed recovery. They can give patients a PRP to improve service tangibility and use digital software solutions to facilitate great outcomes. At the end of the consultation, therapists should always chaperone the patient to reception with a formal handover.

3. **Frequent consultations.** Teach your therapists to be realistic. To effect true behavioural change, they need to train their patients to recover through frequent consultations. The patients will then experience quick benefits, building momentum and commitment.

4. **Caring conversations.** Teach your therapists how to have caring conversations in every consultation. Equip them with the skills they need to discuss the emotional benefits of how the patient will feel when they're better after they've successfully completed therapy.

5. **Mini-hurdles.** Teach your therapists how to break down their patient's SMART goal into mini-hurdles to act as markers to recovery. This is gamification, mapping the patient's progress along their journey, and it must be collaborative between the patient and the therapist as it has a direct improvement on patient motivation, engagement and outcomes.

6. **Nudge theory.** Teach your therapists how to gently nudge patients in the direction they'd like them to take to achieve their aims and goals. Look at many of the common conversion conversations therapists have in the consultation room involving treatment planning, frequency of consultations, product sales, service recommendations, then devise a range of different targeted nudges and have fun practising them through role play.

7. **Membership services.** Look at whether the different services you provide would work as membership programmes, be it Pilates or yoga, massage, acupuncture, dentistry or anything in between. Can you adapt them to fit a recurring-income membership model for the ideal clients in your health business?

When they receive value in every consultation, your patients will reward you and take care of your health business long term. With increased patient engagement, retention and lifetime value, your business will grow exponentially, and loyalty will do a lot of the marketing work for you.

Now let's read on and explore the fifth and final stage of the Practice with Profit Way, Consistent, where you can really boost performance and transform your health business.

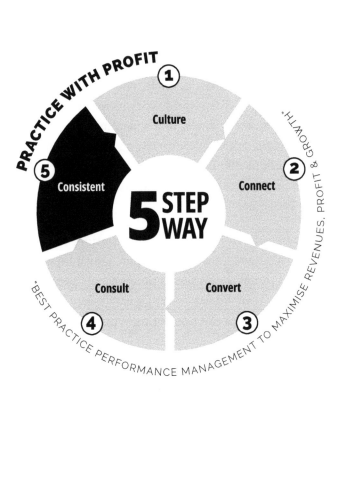

PRACTICE WITH PROFIT

① Culture

② Connect

③ Convert

④ Consult

⑤ Consistent

5 STEP WAY

"BEST PRACTICE PERFORMANCE MANAGEMENT TO MAXIMISE REVENUES, PROFIT & GROWTH."

Six
Step 5 - Consistent

Now we're into the fifth and final stage of the Practice with Profit Way to transform your health business for growth, which is a good time to have a quick recap on how far we've come.

We've gone four layers deep into the consultation room and highlighted the many opportunities for growth and scale that currently exist in your health business. With razor-sharp focus, we've identified the 0.16% of your health business activities that can produce exponential rewards:

Maximise the number of FTE therapists and the time they spend in consultations building valuable patient-therapist relationships with A-star self-paying patients, leading them into a successful course of treatment until they achieve their aims and goals.

Let's split that goal down:

1. **Maximise health business capacity.** In Step 1, Culture, we looked at building a cohesive high-performing therapy team. We explored how to achieve this by maximising your health business capacity and utilisation through the number of FTE therapists and the time they spend helping patients in one-to-one consultations.

2. **Maximise value.** In Step 2, Connect, we outlined how to maximise value by focusing on building patient-therapist relationships with A-star self-funding patients in the consultation room.

3. **Maximise conversion.** In Step 3, Convert, we explored how to maximise converting patients into customers by leading them into a course of therapy as a fundamental starting point for their recovery journey.

4. **Maximise consultations.** In Step 4, Consult, we looked at tips and techniques to maximise the number of patient consultations, adding value, building engagement and retention, guiding your patients successfully to achieving their aims, goals and health transformations.

5. **Maximise performance.** In this final step of the Practice with Profit Way, Consistent, I'll outline a best-practice performance management system to help you build a consistently high-performing therapy team to multiply your revenues, profit and growth. This performance management system entwines with your business culture and goals, delivering a high level of therapist alignment, engagement, motivation and productivity.

When your therapists are doing a great job, your patients will experience great outcomes and you'll increase your health business's profit, growth and scale. I'll outline the practical ways of achieving this by exploring each element of the performance management system in detail:

- KPI dashboard
- Situational leadership
- Strategy and goals
- Peer recognition and support
- Goal, reality, options, will (GROW) performance management tool

I'll focus on you, the leader of your health business, sharing the practical tools to see the subtext of each situation, giving you a repeatable, consistent system to reliably put the metrics into context with best-practice performance management to build sustainable long-term success.

KPI dashboard

By now, you and your therapists should have a good understanding of how the previous four steps of the Practice with Profit Way combine to drive high performance in your health business. At this stage, to manage consistent performance for the long term, I recommend you introduce a measurement system.

Central to these metrics is the 'Goldilocks' KPI dashboard – measure not too many, not too few, just the right amount.

At Practice with Profit, we've learned that too few KPIs mean things remain unclear, too many will negatively affect your therapists' performance, overwhelming them and stressing them. You want to take the middle way, the sweet spot for highly effective performance management.

Let's break down the KPIs down into metrics, arranging them into a dashboard addressing the four main pillars critical to the success of any health business:

- **Growth:** these are simple KPIs that relate to the growth of the business. I'll outline which are the key numbers to indicate health business growth.

- **Efficiency:** these KPIs link to maximising the occupancy of your health business's premises. When you get great staff and develop great services, they're profitable. It's really that simple.

- **Health:** these important KPIs refer to the health of your business. They're the 'soft' metrics: staff motivation and engagement, customer satisfaction, feedback, Google reviews and net promoter scores.

- **Therapy:** these refer to the therapy or operational KPIs within your health business. They're linked to the patient-therapist relationship, retention, average transactional spend, cancellation rate, to name a few.

To be realistic and manage change, you need an understanding of what the key drivers are that influence your business on a quarterly basis. Then with a clear focus, prioritise them on a monthly or quarterly basis and improve them for growth.

We'll now go into detail on the KPIs from each pillar that make up your performance dashboard, exploring how they interrelate and how you can use them to monitor and improve the overall profitability and growth of your health business.

Growth KPIs

Growth KPIs include your:

- BHAG
- Revenue
- Revenue per employee (RPE)
- Revenue and sales mix

BHAG

This KPI references your BHAG, which sets the vision for the team to 'live' your values and behaviours to achieve your one single business goal. Your BHAG is defined by your health business's purpose and becomes your North Star to guide champion performance.

At goPhysio, our purpose is to 'Help people live a healthy, active, positive life, pain and injury free.' From this, our BHAG, which we term our 20:20 vision, is to 'Achieve 100,000 consultations by a specified time.'

Your BHAG is a cohesive goal that sets the direction everyone in the business can work towards on a patient-by-patient basis, daily and weekly, from minimising cancellations to maximising conversions and health transformations.

Revenue

When you're analysing revenue growth, the best KPI is to look at the cumulative revenue over the last fifty-two weeks and plot the trend. This provides a clear indication of whether the business is growing, plateauing or declining. The cumulative aspect smooths out the seasonal trends, enabling you to clearly see at a glance what's happening. Keep your revenue KPIs up to date every week and the trend will become clear.

You can plot total revenue for the whole business, but also split it down per service to see the sales mix. Often, you will see that the effects on the cumulative trends per service are linked to capacity. Capacity, or utilisation, is generally the biggest constraint to growth in a health business, so it's not a coincidence we covered it in step one of the Practice with Profit Way.

I'd also advise you to look at the cumulative revenue per therapist to see if their level of clinical mastery is tailored to the health business. Revenue is an overall trend and highly valuable when you're doing performance reviews, planning new services or reviewing pricing.

RPE

As Daniel Priestley explains in his best-selling book, 24 *Assets* (2017), all businesses exist on an axis of team size and RPE, so RPE needs to be an integral part of your KPI dashboard as you seek to maximise it. It depends on many factors: your health business's specialism, it's positioning, your customer segment, pricing structure and sales mix, to name a few.

Revenue is good to grow, but it needs to be profitable revenue. Keep an eye on RPE as it is a great way to highlight and grow your most profitable services.

Here's an example:

- **Masseuse:** billing @ £50 per hour, equates to an annual revenue of £92,800
- **Physio:** billing @ £90 per hour, equates to an annual revenue of £167,000
- **Dentist:** billing @ £200 per hour, equates to an annual revenue of £371,000

I'm accounting for individuals working a forty-hour week, having twenty days' annual leave, eight bank holidays per year and utilisation at 80%.

On paper, these revenues are quite respectable, but as health-business leaders, you'll know these figures are hard to achieve because:

- Consistent 80% utilisation is a challenge
- It takes at least six months of investment to on-board and train new employees to become productive team members and bill at those RPEs

Nevertheless, a minimum annual RPE target for each therapist to be profitable should be between £110,000 to £130,000 (depending on their profession or specialism).

Keeping an eye on RPE also helps monitor staff creep, keeping your business efficient and lean. Staff creep refers to when you expand your team to include the salaries of employees in non-income generating roles, which will reduce the RPE and profitability of your business.

To help illustrate this point, have a look at the table below. It's modelled on a super-efficient, lean lifestyle health business with an annual revenue of £120,000 per therapist.

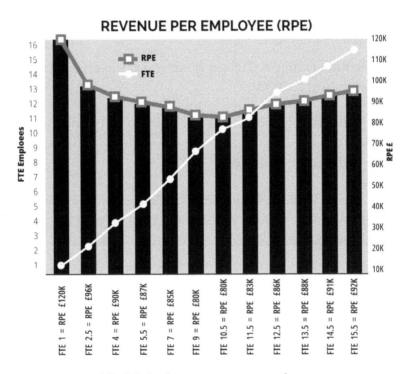

Lifestyle business revenue per employee

Health-business leaders who don't set a strategic plan to maximise their RPE as they grow their business and non-billing team will see their RPE and profits shrink. Ultimately, the more non-billing team members you recruit as you grow, the lower your overall RPE. So, as you grow without a clear and focused plan on steadily increasing your RPE through the Practice with Profit Way, your most profitable days with high RPE will be a distant memory.

Revenue and sales mix

This KPI helps you identify your mix of services and their profitability. As your profits are affected dramatically by your revenue and sales mix, when you look at the mix cumulatively over time, you can see if you are getting the right types of sales which contribute most to your profits and growth. By having a clear focus on your most profitable services, you'll be able to maximise the profitability of your health business.

Efficiency

To understand the constraints that affect your health business, you need these two KPIs as your health-business efficiency pillar:

- Therapist utilisation
- Capacity utilisation

Therapist utilisation

This relates to the percentage of time your therapists spend in one-to-one appointments, helping patients achieve their aims and goals. At goPhysio, our target is that 80% of our therapists' contracted hours should be spent in one-to-one consultations, classes or any other billable activity in which they're helping patients. The remaining 20% consists of cancellations, DNAs (did not attends), admin, meetings, training, projects and service development. It doesn't sound like a lot, but within a forty-hour week, 20% equates to eight hours per week per therapist.

Within the realms of possibility, you need to maximise therapist utilisation through your performance management system. Aim for the consistently high-performing yet realistic target of 80% of each therapist's time being spent in billable activity in which they're helping patients. This after all is their purpose; it's what they've trained to do and the reason your health business exists. Therapist utilisation relates directly to how much time their patients want to spend in their company, solving health issues. It relates to how much their patients believe in them as the solution to their health problems, so it's a combined measure of your therapists' clinical mastery and productivity.

Capacity utilisation

This relates to the occupancy of the billable space within your health business, eg the consultation rooms or studios. This is a massive constraint for most health businesses as they have specific levels of capacity.

Being able to track your levels of spare capacity tells you how well your business is doing. It's critical to maximise the utilisation of these spaces to maximise revenue and profits. At Practice with Profit, we aim for a realistic yet sustainable utilisation of capacity target of greater than 80%.

Understanding these metrics, measuring and managing them, changed my mindset. Hopefully with this new understanding, you too can move forward, develop and implement a plan to focus on what you can control to achieve your business goals, so I urge you to discuss these health-business constraints with your therapists.

Help your therapists develop a clear focus on the important elements that they can control, day-to-day, in each of their roles, so when you implement great services into your business, they will be profitable. These two KPIs are vital metrics to track over time to ensure you're getting the best ROI from the two biggest expenses in your health business: your people and premises.

Health

This pillar references the health of the business in terms of staff motivation levels and customer satisfaction. In other words, the soft metrics.

Staff motivation

The motivation level of your team is the simplest barometer for the health of your business. Team motivation levels are dynamic and need to be regularly monitored and reviewed.

At practice with profit we use an online diagnostic motivational interviewing tool that is based on three well-established theories of motivation by Maslow, Schein and Enneagram. It's licensed to people like us around the world who want to make a motivational difference. By implementing this motivational interview process as part of your therapists' development programme, you can gain clear metrics on each team member's motivation levels as a percentage. Then you can devise an action plan to ensure your therapists remain engaged and motivated.

Customer satisfaction

At Practice with Profit, we advocate regular gathering of customer feedback at key touchpoints in the patients' recovery journey. Don't hassle your patients with surveys; keep feedback as simple as patients pressing a screen on leaving the building.

The Net Promoter score (NPS) is a simple, reliable way to measure feedback. Extensive research into this tool has identified that an NPS of 8.5 or more is a leading indicator of a high-growth company (Net Promoter, 2017).

Therapy

Over the last twenty years, I've researched and implemented many different KPIs for therapists, so I've now reached a point where I've measured enough behind the scenes to be able to monitor trends. They help me identify how effective my business's therapists are at solving the problems I've employed them to solve.

These KPIs are closely aligned to the therapists', patients' and health business's purpose and BHAG. They are forward- and future-facing, not historically focused. They are not used as a stick to deliver change. Instead, they guide the behaviours and performance required to achieve the BHAG.

These KPIs consistent of:

- **BHAG tracker:** monthly feedback on progress towards achieving the BHAG
- **Conversions:** the percentage of patients who completed a successful recovery plan and achieved their goals
- **Therapist utilisation:** a measurement of the total percentage of the time a therapist spends in direct income-generating activity with a patient

This four-pillar KPI system for your health business is guided by your purpose and champion performance. Essentially, if your therapists are doing a great job, their patients will enjoy great outcomes, which will increase revenue, profitability, growth and scale for your health business.

Feedback

When you've implemented the four KPI pillars within your health business, displaying them in a monthly dashboard, what's next? What's the best way to use them to effect positive change aligned with the aims and goals of the stakeholders: your therapists, patients and health business?

It is true that what you can measure, you can manage, and that feedback is the breakfast of champions, but it's crucial to understand that in a health business, managing by numbers alone doesn't work. It leads to fear, anxiety, defensiveness, which dramatically limit therapists' performance, both individually and as a team.

Having learned from our mistakes, we at Practice with Profit recommend that the directors monitor the four KPI pillars on a monthly basis, analysing trends, putting them into context through discussions with our lead therapist and then making course corrections. The team is given timely performance feedback via a monthly KPI dashboard, which is referenced in quarterly performance development meetings and team communications. If the numbers go off track, the directors manage therapist performance by exception. When trends are consistently off by more than 5%, the directors meet the lead therapist and discuss the way forward.

We might vary the KPI targets per therapist, based on their competencies. Overall, it's all about the people, whether they have the right individual components of:

- **Attitude:** visions, purpose, values, work ethic, morals, engagement, motivation

- **Capability:** do they have any training requirements to develop clinical mastery tailored for a health business?

- **Capacity:** are they working to the level of capacity that is reasonable to do the job and help their patients? If they're working below capacity, there is a problem, but it's important to remember that people can be working under capacity due to inefficiency or perfectionism.

At Practice with Profit, we're aware change will take longer than we'd like. In cases of underperformance, the directors have discussions with the clinical lead, who delivers valuable context from an operational standpoint. This process enables us to look closely at the key drivers that influence the therapists and business on a monthly and quarterly basis and implement the relevant changes.

Situational leadership

A situational style of leadership and performance management means you adapt your style depending on the attitudes, capability and capacity of the therapist – leading, directing, coaching and supporting them through each of the four quadrants shown in the illustration until they become unconsciously competent in the specific task or skill.

1
Directing
This involves training the therapist who has a lot of enthusiasm to achieve the result, but not much actual ability

2
Coaching & Guiding
For those therapists who have been in the business a while, but may have started to lose confidence and motivation

4
Delegate
We then delegate to the technically competent and confident team members who consistently achieve their targets

3
Peer Support
This is for therapists whose technical ability has improved but who still lack confidence or ability to achieve the results consistently

Situational leadership

This approach helps the business leader tailor their style to the specific situation and the level of competency of the therapist in the task. It's a structured pathway to guide therapists in developing clinical mastery while supporting them adequately to achieve their targets and goals. At Practice with Profit, we recommend you implement this process in a variety of formal and informal ways:

- **Informal situational leadership** is a great way to motivate your therapists to start delegating small tasks while coaching and guiding them on a day-to-day basis through the four stages of the model in the illustration. Before you delegate any task, it's important to put it through the filter of situational leadership and assess the gap in your therapists' capability and ability. Clearly communicate:

  » **Task:** what does success look like?

  » **Feedback loop:** clarify what they understand, eg *'Just so I know I've explained myself clearly and I've not missed any information, can you explain what you understand, the expectation of the task, what you need to achieve?'*

- **Formal situational leadership** covers more formal ways to help develop your therapist's competencies. This could include:

  » Weekly open-door sessions with the therapy lead

  » Fortnightly case reviews

  » Monthly peer shadowing sessions

  » Quarterly personal-development interviews

In true coaching style, ask questions of your therapists rather than tell them the answer, empowering them to take ownership of the solution, their productivity and the results.

This is easier said than done, especially when the therapy leader or business director has a vested interest in the outcome of the results, which is why involving a third-party experienced coach is highly rewarding in bringing about transformative change. At Practice with Profit, we avoid negative language such as 'but, 'however', 'let me explain', 'with the greatest respect', removing barriers that are preventing our therapists from achieving their goals by framing the issue(s) with a question:

- How do we...?
- How can we...?
- How could we...?

CASE STUDY

Here's a simple example of how this works in practice. Let's say a therapist is great clinically, but lacks the relevant communication skills and is having difficulty with the sales aspect of their role. They're unable to convert a large percentage of their patients into customers signing up to a successful course of treatment. The therapist is experiencing high cancellation rates and low patient retention. Despite their best intentions, they're failing to help their patients. Essentially, they are not performing in the role or solving the problems you've employed them to solve.

As therapy lead or health-business owner, you have some options to help them succeed in their role:

- You could minimise the transactional aspect of their service with the addition of treatment packages. Teach them to sell the solution once, eg sell one block of seven sessions rather than an ongoing transaction on a consultation-by-consultation basis. Essentially, patients want the result not the process, so sell them the result. Sell them the outcome.

- If a treatment package is too much change for the therapist to take on board at once, teach them how to sell themselves as the solution naturally, authentically, in alignment with their motivations and values. This is where understanding the individual motivators of the therapist is crucial to finding the triggers to elicit change.

Imagine your toughest challenge as a health-business leader: the altruistic therapist. Their tendency to self-sacrifice, ostensibly for the benefit of their patients, is limiting your success. You need to discover a high motivator for them, for example the desire to become an expert in their field, then approach improving their motivation for change through their own high motivator.

You can do this by entering into a dialogue like this one:

THERAPY LEAD: You know that in this health business we're looking to give the best treatment to help patients successfully achieve their aims and goals?

THERAPIST: Yeah, of course.

THERAPY LEAD: So if money was no object, to truly resolve this patient's problem, achieving their aims and goals 100% and preventing reoccurrence, how many consultations would they need?

THERAPIST: If money was no object, wow! Maybe eight to ten consultations.

THERAPY LEAD: OK, so on average, what would that look like for the vast majority of your patients across the board?

THERAPIST: Maybe six to seven consultations on average.

THERAPY LEAD: OK, but when we look at your KPIs, we're seeing a totally different trend with 40% of your patients leaving after just one to two consultations. Is it fair to say that those patients are disappearing still suffering with health problems, having not achieved their aims and goals?

THERAPIST: Yeah, I suppose so.

THERAPY LEAD: I know you trained to help people, you're really knowledgeable and experienced and want to make a difference, but you're not using your expertise with 40% of your patients as they're not achieving their aims and goals.

THERAPIST: Hmmm…

THERAPIST LEAD: So how can you get your knowledge, experience, skills out of your head and communicate them in a non-technical manner so all your patients commit to a successful treatment plan and achieve great outcomes?

The coaching session then follows on with the therapist presenting options and solutions to boost their performance, gaining ownership and commitment to the action plan. It's a re-education process led by the therapy lead and/or coaching expert, structured around what action steps are required to help improve patient retention. The whole coaching conversation needs to be clearly linked to the health business's purpose, BHAG, and ultimately the therapist's role as an employee of your health business.

Many health-business leaders adopt a directive approach, developing prescriptive treatment pathways to exert some control over their therapists, standardise care and improve performance. Prescriptive care pathways have their role for therapists in the first and second quadrants ('Directing' and 'Coaching and guiding') of the situational leadership model in the illustration. These are the inexperienced, newly qualified or new recruits to your health business who lack the ability or confidence to achieve the results you want consistently. They're also useful with those therapists who require more direction, coaching, support and guidance on how you operate as a health business and what best practice looks like.

With more experienced therapists well trained in the Practice with Profit Way, those in quadrants three or four ('Peer support' and 'Delegate', I recommend you only use care pathways as a quick guide. There are dangers with care pathways that if you use them indiscriminately, they can stifle autonomy, mastery and purpose, which has the undesired effect of therapist demotivation, disengagement and drop-out.

Strategy and goals

At Practice with Profit, we encourage health-business leaders to review their strategy on a quarterly basis, implementing a ninety-day planning format to identify:

- Where they are now. Are they on track?
- What needs to be changed, refined or modified to achieve targets?

They can then set the quarterly agenda to achieve the desired goals, reviewing the therapists' performance and confidence levels on a monthly basis with regards to changing and adapting the plan as appropriate. Finally, they feed the most important messages – the priorities that will move the needle most – down to the therapy team.

It's important to understand what great outcomes look like and why measuring is vital to success. Therapists need to be clear on what they are doing for the business in terms of consistency of KPIs.

A big issue can be lack of consistent, regular feedback in a format that therapists can understand. This is a crucial component to a winning formula. Without the feedback and relevant course correction, it's impossible to build momentum and improve. It's all about the marginal gains; there isn't one quick fix or magic pill. All five steps of the Practice with Profit Way when combined will multiply the performance, revenue, profit, growth and scale of your health business.

By adopting the principles laid out in this fifth step, you provide clear performance feedback to your therapists on a regular and timely basis in a consistent format they can understand, with no surprises. It's important there are no sudden changes or surprises as therapists can easily feel overwhelmed if there are. With surprises, they tend to freeze and go on the defensive.

If they have too much to think about or there is constant change, therapists become stressed, resulting in poor performance. They just want to care for their patients in the best possible way, so as a leader your role is to simply enable them to make the best decisions for their patients in the context of a health business.

Peer recognition and support

Peer shadowing system

Once a month, it's a good idea for therapists to shadow a colleague in the consultation room and review their performance against all the steps of the Practice with Profit Way. Afterwards, they schedule a fifteen-minute feedback session with their colleague on what went well and areas for improvement that would give the quickest boost to performance. It's all done with the business, patients and therapists' best interests at heart to enable you to continuously improve your professional development and performance.

This approach to peer shadowing has many positives. It's a successful consultation-room-focused clinical performance-management system that assesses and improves all the critical components of the Practice with Profit Way. It doesn't rely on management involvement and there is great buy-in from therapists as the feedback comes from like-minded and trusted peers, rather than another directive from above.

Recognition and reward system

I also recommend you implement a peer-to-peer recognition and reward system. This is vital to encourage and reward everyone within the business for living your core values and behaviours, but it won't happen on its own. It's the team leader's role to recognise and reward as and when the right behaviours happen in real-time, making sure the recognition is consistent and authentic. Culture is not a fad. To embed your values and guide behaviours deeply within your health business as 'the way we do things here' takes organisation, consistency and effort. You need to implement a clear and simple communication system to give positive, timely feedback on all the vital day-to-day therapist activities and behaviours that contribute to achieving your BHAG.

That means noticing all the small day-to-day actions that go towards achieving your goals and giving timely recognition in the form of thanks. At Practice with Profit, we use www.peoplehr.com. This software keeps track of the many routine HR tasks in one handy dashboard. We choose an award aligned to one of our core values, for example 'Helpful and Caring', then write a brief thank you recognising the therapist's action. But we don't cut and paste it; the thank you needs to be individualised and authentic, explaining how the therapist lived the values while helping their patient.

Helpful & Caring 5

" Mary, I heard you sent a patient of yours a text over the weekend asking how their long run went in preparation for their marathon training. They were really thankful for that special touch and that is certainly going above and beyond. Thank you for going that extra mile, fantastic work. "

Mary received thanks from
Fiona Moir - Mon, 11 Mar 2019

Thank you – above and beyond

In the early days of adopting this system, most of the thanks come from the directors and therapy lead, but within a few weeks, the team will start using it more and more frequently to recognise and reward their peers. Peer-to-peer recognition is a great system to build strong motivation and connection between colleagues at work as therapists can become turned off by even genuine messages of thanks coming from the top. The cynics are sceptical of there being an alternative motive, but not when the messages of thanks come from their colleagues and peers.

It gets better. At the end of each month, the system we use at Practice with Profit totals each therapist's individual thanks. The therapist with the highest number of thank-you messages from their peers wins the coveted 'team member of the month' title and chooses a reward from a range of £50 vouchers sealed in envelopes.

A great tip here is that the best rewards are those the therapist can share with a partner, family member or friend. It could be for a meal in a restaurant, a trip to the cinema or day out. As long as it's something they can share with a loved one, it further reinforces the recognition. Then at end of year, you can go a step further and have a 'team member of the year' award in which the winner gets an extra day's leave, the runner up a half day for the next year.

At Practice with Profit, we find that a fun monthly reward and recognition system is a positive way to reinforce the values and behaviours our therapists need to live to achieve our health-business vision. This gives us the best opportunity of collectively achieving our goals. Overall, it's a great way of aligning our business purpose, vision and values with our therapists' intrinsic motivators and purpose.

By involving everyone in the award ceremony, you can recognise behaviour and achievement within the team, aligning everyone's energy towards a common goal. Think of it as a sticky chart for adults.

Motivation

The motivation level of your therapists is an indicator of the health of your business. Motivation is dynamic; it changes over time, and it's the line manager's responsibility to identify and react to these changes. Having a full understanding of what employees want to achieve as individuals and showing them how to do it helps to build a strong, engaged and high-performing team.

Health-business leaders need to be committed to creating an environment to encourage motivation. Motivation is highly critical in building a team. If you're a visionary leader, if you're involved in planning and thinking about the next three to five years of growth and development of your health business, you need to interweave motivation with performance management. You need to be continuously thinking about team motivation, planning and implementing the next two to three steps. The first step is to give your therapists the time out of work to explore their motivations, investing in their training and self-development so they can gain a good understanding of themselves while using their brains and getting something rewarding from the process in return.

GROW performance management tool

In successful health businesses, professional leaders have specific duties to improve company performance. At Practice with Profit, we help implement a performance-management measurement system that consists of:

- **SMART KPIs:** measure operational goals that link to performance
- **Competencies:** soft measures of the skills and goals over a longer period

We help leaders implement a monthly therapist KPI dashboard that measures and monitors the critical results for performance management. Therapists' KPIs are streamlined down to three critical metrics relevant to each person's role and responsibilities. These are the KPIs they need to be measured against to achieve top performance within the company, and they need to be SMART:

- **Specific:** what needs to be done?

- **Measurable:** if the numbers go off track by 5%, put them into context with leadership team discussions and make course corrections.

- **Achievable:** review what's been happening historically with the essential metrics, calculate averages, elevate them slightly as stretch targets and make them the therapists' initial objectives. The targets need to be realistic and achievable to keep things positive. Then when your therapists are performing and hitting the benchmarks consistently, increase the target in small increments.

- **Relevant:** KPIs must always be aligned to the organisational goals and objectives.

- **Time-bound:** targets need a timeline or deadline.

Central to performance management is holding each individual accountable to their objectives and goals to ensure that they're achieving them. To do this, balance the organisational goals with the operational goals in collaboration with the therapists. This collaboration is important in gaining therapist ownership and accountability, which is often the biggest issue with performance management. Involving the therapists improves their individual responsibility for their performance; it's a powerful thing.

Each role within your business should also have a softer competency framework to measure performance against.

This is made up of eight to ten competencies critical to each role with a simple three-point rating system:

1. Poor performance, consistently below expectations

2. Solid performance, meets and exceeds

3. High performance, consistently above expectations

The communication process you use to provide feedback on the findings of your performance management system is critical. At Practice with Profit, we recommend you implement the GROW model:

- Goal:

    » What do you want to achieve?

    » What's your timeline to achieve it?

- Reality:

    » Validate and be aware of the current situation

- Options

    » What are the options or solutions for achieving what you want to achieve?

    » What are the challenges or problems you need to overcome?

- Will:

    » Test each individual's commitment, rate it out of ten

    » Describe the action steps to achieve what you want to achieve

This model is a coaching and support system, based on structured open questions, discussions and input from the therapist. The therapist is central to the process and the solution, developing autonomy and ownership.

Tangible takeaways

In the final stage of the Practice with Profit way, we've come full circle and looked at how to transform your health business with a consistently high-performing therapy team. We've aligned your performance-management system with current best-practice principles in leadership and motivational change.

Here are six tangible takeaways to implement into your health business. Choose between one and two takeaways to introduce into your business per quarter as part of your best-practice performance-management system.

1. **KPI dashboard.** Develop your leadership KPI dashboard, measuring some metrics on a monthly basis, others on a quarterly basis. Then develop a streamlined version for your therapists to include BHAG tracker, revenue mix, individual therapist utilisation, overall utilisation of the health business's capacity and percentage of patients successfully completing a recovery plan and achieving their goals. There are other therapist-specific KPIs that I've used over the years, but in true 80/20 style, I've included the 20% that will give 80% of the results. Remember not to measure too many KPIs or too few.

2. **Analyse the four KPI pillars.** As the team leader, you're well equipped to develop motivated employees

with high performance who contribute to the overall financial objectives of your health business, so analyse the four KPI pillars on a monthly basis and monitor them for trends. If the numbers go off track by 5%, put them into context with leadership team discussions and make course corrections.

3. **Situational leadership.** Develop a situational leadership style around best-practice coaching principles. Implement this process into your health business in formal and informal ways.

4. **Personal-development interviews.** Implement quarterly development interviews with your therapists based around motivational interviewing techniques and their competencies. Develop SMART goals within the GROW framework to build an engaged high-performance team to achieve the growth objectives of your business.

5. **Peer shadowing.** Schedule time for each therapist to shadow a colleague in the consultation room and assess their performance against the steps of the Practice with Profit Way. Afterwards, the two therapists meet for an honest feedback session.

6. **Reward and recognition.** Implement a peer-to-peer reward and recognition system in your health business to give day-to-day thanks to your team for living the core values and behaviours required to achieve your business goals.

In this chapter, I've outlined a best-practice performance-management system that delivers a high level of therapist engagement, motivation and productivity. When your therapists are doing a great job, your patients enjoy great outcomes and your health business enjoys increased revenue, profitability, growth and scale. Implement the five-step Practice with Profit Way to multiply your profits and grow your practice with less stress and more freedom.

Conclusion
Breaking Down The Barriers

As an expert clinician and health-business leader for over twenty years, I understand that with the correct knowledge, experience and systems, you can grow a profitable practice that relies on maximising your number of FTE therapists and the time they spend in consultations building valuable patient-therapist relationships with A-star self-funding patients, converting them into customers who follow a course of therapy until they achieve their aims and goals.

In this chapter, I'll summarise the barriers you may be facing to following the Practice with Profit Way. These profit barriers will be in one of three main areas:

- Your therapists' mindset

- A broken business model

- Low ROI in your people and capital assets

When they're left unaddressed, these factors can cause you as the business leader to descend into a cycle of despair.

We'll calculate the costs of not addressing and solving these issues. We'll then look at the many opportunities that currently exist within your health business for profit, growth and scale when you implement a winning strategy and system. The Practice with Profit Way will solve these issues once and for all.

Therapist mindset

All roads that lead to health-business transformation start with your therapists' mindset. If you fail to address common mindset issues, you'll be forever stuck managing a misaligned, disengaged, poor-performing therapy team that doesn't achieve your goals.

Miscommunication

Your therapists are likely to be oblivious to the costs associated with running a bricks-and-mortar health business and the levels of performance you require from them for profitability and long-term success. Many don't consider sales part of their job description; they simply know that they're working in a health business which needs to make a profit. They're blind to the crucial role they play; how their thoughts, feelings and behaviours in the consultation room have a dramatic effect on the health business's profitability and success. They find the idea of developing the commercial knowledge to succeed painful as it clashes with their caring side, which is a major problem for health businesses in the modern age.

Therapists are concerned primarily with being the best they can be for both patient and business success, but often they neglect to develop interpersonal, commercial and problem-solving skills. No doubt, your therapists' clinical skills are the platform on which you build a sustainable health business, but without the business, communication and problem-solving skills working in unison with their core clinical skills, they litter their conversations with technical jargon, communicating in an ineffective and confusing way.

When this happens, the patient becomes confused and only hears snippets of information. They don't understand clearly how the therapist can help them solve their health issues and achieve their aims and goals. As a result, they take the low-risk option, often making poor decisions for their welfare as a result. They either sign up to a watered-down treatment plan or fail to commit to a successful course of treatment and are never seen again.

Either result is clearly to the detriment of the therapist's personal and professional development, patient transforma-tions and health business success. To increase your ROI, you need to commercialise and monetise your therapists' clinical knowledge, so your patients and health business can reap the full rewards.

Evidence base limitations

It's important your therapists develop knowledge and under-standing of the evidence base and use it responsibly to shape clinical practice and facilitate optimum patient outcomes, but it's equally important they understand that it's only one type of knowledge. As outlined by Mark Jones and Darren Rivett in their excellent book *Clinical Reasoning for Manual Therapists* (2003), to develop clinical mastery, understand and successfully treat patients' health problems fully, therapists need to have a rich organisation of three different types of knowledge: the evidence base (propositional), professional (craft) and personal or life experience.

The reality is that identical patient problems do not exist in the real world, in your health business, in the consultation room. Knowledge of the evidence base – through research articles and scientific papers – alone does not provide your therapists with all the information they need in any individual patient encounter. It doesn't paint the whole picture of the patient. The evidence doesn't equip your therapists with the best treatment for 'Mrs Jones' there and then in the consultation room, treating her particular condition, on that particular day, at that particular stage of healing and recovery. It will not help your therapists lead her into a successful course of treatment to achieve her unique aims and goals.

Consequently, knowledge gained from the therapist's clinical and life experience (experiential learning) is just as important as that gained from science and evidence.

Our human experience is subjective. We perceive the world through our five senses that input messages into our nervous system. Pure objectivity doesn't exist. The now famous double-slit experiment that the Buddhist monk Chopra and physicist Kafatos discuss in their thought-provoking book *You Are the Universe* (2017) has taught us that once we have observed or measured something, we change it. They go a step further and explain that no two people see the world exactly alike and no one can claim to know what is 'really' real as long as their brain, with its complex set of physiological and psychological filters, is their window on the universe. You cannot step outside your nervous system.

So, in a clinical setting, a smile, the language your therapists use, the service they provide, the messages they give directly into their patients' nervous system are all subjective, no matter how much research they've read or how evidence based they think it is.

Obviously, their treatment approach needs to be as current and clinically reasoned as possible, but it's only one type of knowledge, a sliver of reality. It isn't the be-all and end-all, and the belief that it is can so often be to the detriment of patients' experiences and outcomes. Ultimately your therapists are real people trying to help other real people. As Diane Lee expertly put it in her book, *The Pelvic Girdle* (2010):

'Clinical practice will always be a blend of science and art with a healthy dose of logic and reasoning.'

When we look at building a profitable practice through the evidence-base lens, we can understand why many health businesses are relatively unprofitable. In the absence of career-long reflective practice, high patient mileage and experience, therapists give the evidence base too much influence on their decision-making and treatment-planning process. It stifles their lateral-thinking, creativity, problem-identification and problem-solving skills, often leading to a conflict in their heads with uncertainty and indecision seeming to be the safe evidence-based option.

This has a dramatic effect on therapists' ability to identify and solve complex problems and provide valuable health transformations. Infrequent sessions with patients, slow progress, disengagement and poor outcomes all negatively affect your therapists', patients' and health business's success.

Assumptions and hang-ups

Your therapists and patients bring plenty of assumptions, hang-ups, paradigms and flawed thinking into the consultation room. They're mainly price and not value focused, which means they greet any reference to pricing or profit with cynicism.

To many therapists, the idea of developing valuable relationships at the core of a health business for profit and growth seems like a contentious issue: the business of gain from people's pain. But over the last twenty+ years, I've learned that failing to build valuable patient-therapist relationships in the consultation room results in low levels of patient engagement and retention, poor outcomes, and lost revenue and profit.

Broken business model

With these prevailing mindset issues in play, is it any wonder that many therapists have mediocre sales skills in which a transactional business model dominates, often leading to low conversions, engagement and retention, poor patient outcomes and short lifetime values? As a result, healthcare businesses become predominately new-patient focused.

This is a flawed business model that is impossible to grow.

Mediocre sales skills

It's no secret that many therapists have poor sales skills and a strong aversion to developing these skills. It's what I term the clinical sales paradox.

Therapists are caring and well-meaningful professionals who are trained to help people, but they have a deep aversion to developing sales skills. What many don't realise is that they require great sales skills to help people in deep, trans-formative ways. They lack the high-quality knowledge and training in professional sales skills to move patients to health transformations.

Therapists often harbour an unfounded but deep-seated fear of being perceived as 'too commercial' by colleagues and peers. As a result, they settle for a safe but ineffective sales strategy, with non-committal language full of ambiguities, which is totally at odds with their aims and goals.

Low patient retention

Confused patients have difficulty seeing the value of the solu-tions their therapists offer and become hesitant and indecisive. Often, they then make ill-informed decisions for their health and welfare. They fail to commit to a successful recovery plan until completion, instead disengaging prematurely without reaching their goals. A large percentage opt for the low risk, the status quo, putting up with long-term suffering and disability. They vote with their wallet, never to return, which of course leads to poor patient outcomes.

When a health business adopts the routine practice of under-servicing their current customers with low engagement and retention, it results in lost patients, lost revenues and lost profits.

Employment versus self-employment

A question I'm often asked by health-business leaders is 'Should our therapists be employed or self-employed?' It's no coincidence that I'm asked this by the health-business leaders whose therapists are all self-employed associates.

Examining the evidence, I've come to the conclusion that the practices with self-employed therapists are the more unprofitable. Self-employed therapists are paid a percentage fee of up to 60% of revenue generated. That leaves only 40% of revenue to cover all the other associated capital and running costs of the business. Once non-clinical salaries are paid, there is simply no profit.

This self-employed approach to business is not a profitable business model; it's just a JOB (just over broke) model. It often results in the practice leader being chained to the consultation room, working flat-out in the business to break even on the crippling overheads, too busy to lead their team.

If you're using the self-employed business model, you need to ask yourself the question, 'Who is working for whom?' You're likely to discover that in reality, the health business is working for the self-employed contractors, taking all the risks with rising overheads and no profit, while keeping these therapists in the lifestyle they are accustomed to.

I understand that on the surface, self-employed contractors might seem like the easy option to many health-business owners. It is often far from that. It can be counterproductive to developing an aligned, engaged and cohesive therapy team, which is a fundamental element to building a profitable practice for growth and scale.

Most motivated and aligned therapists I have met who are living the business's values, working positively towards achieving the business's vision, are employed, not self-employed. Since my health business abandoned the self-employed contractor model a few years ago, it has grown from strength to strength with cost of services below 30% and a gross profit above 30%.

Be warned, though, it's not easy to find FTE therapists, especially from the scarce talent pool we are currently experiencing in the health and wellbeing industry. It takes a transition period with a great recruitment process where you're employing on vision, culture and values. Thankfully, my business is now out the other end with a great team of motivated, aligned, purposeful therapists, recruited based on a culture and values match with the business.

I'd strongly recommend you get professional guidance and help from someone who's been through it and understands the hazards and pitfalls. Employed therapists are the only way to build long-term profitability, success and growth for all stakeholders.

Free healthcare

In the UK, having the government-funded NHS as a competitor can be a major issue for any health business. The NHS provides similar services for free while running at a loss of £20 billion per annum, which has massive implications on the strategy, differentiation and positioning of any health business.

Unfortunately, many health businesses try to compete on price, which is foolish. If your only differentiator is price, you're doomed to fail as you can't compete with free. Instead, as a health-business leader, you need to realise there are many other costs involved with using the NHS that are not directly related to money. These 'costs' can include time spent on waiting lists for appointments, time taken off work due to limited appointment availability, appointment inconvenience and lack of choice, travelling and parking costs, lack of facilities and services, not being able to choose your therapist, infrequent appointments. You get the idea.

Do yourself, your therapists, patients and health business a favour: value yourself more. Differentiate and position your health business to avoid a race to the bottom, lost revenues and profits.

Low ROI

In a health business your people are the second largest investment after capital expense. By people, I mean your therapists and their patient-therapist relationships at the core of your health business. The reality is without their know-how, it's difficult to grow and scale.

Many health businesses experience a low ROI in their current team, marketing activities or any new venture or business initiative. It's lose-lose for all involved, which has a major impact on a health business's strategy and positioning. But why is this?

People and capital assets

Health-business owners and leaders often think the best way to scale and grow their business is through investment in new, innovative strategies and services. I'm reminded of a recent visit to an orthopaedic consultant's office. While we were discussing our businesses, he enquired, 'What equipment have you got at your place?' A simple statement, but the implication is that the success of a health business is based on its equipment: the shiny, tangible objects in the consultation room.

The fact is the success of a health business is based in the people: the therapists and patients who use the equipment. Health businesses that just invest in the best facilities, equipment and technology, while failing to invest in their therapists, never quite live up to forecasts or predictions. They suffer a long-time lag before they see any ROI from new initiatives or service developments.

The real issue is that most health business's investments are not centred around therapists with great interpersonal problem-solving or sales skills. This is why they fail to realise a significant ROI.

New-patient focus

With low patient retention, health businesses become new-patient focused. The leaders mistakenly assume that the attrition is due to clinical factors as their therapists are doing the best jobs they can technically. They're blind to the benefits of investing in developing the soft skills, the interpersonal and problem-solving skills, as a fast-track way to profit and growth. Instead, rather than address the cause of the patient attrition, they treat the symptoms. They increase the marketing investment while under-servicing their current patients, wasting their marketing money. All the while, they're unaware that growth opportunities are already there, hidden within their business.

Performance management

Unsure of which key metrics to measure and manage, many health businesses confuse their therapists with regular updates and changes to the KPI dashboards. Confused therapists become defensive and demotivated, and their performance suffers.

Discounted contracts

It's common for health businesses to hire therapists on technical skills, but without developing great interpersonal and problem-solving skills among their therapists, health businesses fail to realise their full ROI.

Unable to leverage their business, many leaders adapt their strategy and business model. They tender for discounted work through the many private medical or intermediary companies. They outsource or subcontract therapy to self-employed contractors, associates or other health businesses.

True, this delegates the responsibility and the headaches, but it also decreases the business's margin. This approach massively dilutes revenue, profit and growth for all. With reduced revenue and increased administration, profits plummet. It often becomes a race to the bottom between competitors, which third parties exploit. This throws the well-meaning health-business leader into a cycle of despair. They have to sell their services more and more cheaply, becoming hopelessly squeezed on profit.

Cycle of despair

The combined effect of the barriers I've outlined makes it extremely difficult to scale and grow any health service or business that has people and relationships at its core. The warning sign of lost opportunities is that the unprofitable health business becomes caught up in a race to bottom, which I predict will become more and more common. We will then have a crowd of commoditised health businesses providing poor services at rock-bottom prices with minimal margins, barely surviving in a place where extinction always looms.

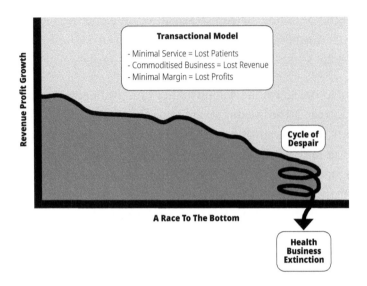

Unprofitable practice

Lost opportunity

The cycle of despair is characterised by ineffective leadership, stress, lack of control and career stagnation. A health business suffering in the cycle of despair will experience:

- Lost patients
- Lost revenue
- Lost profits
- Lost team
- Lack of growth

As the business leader, you'll find yourself confused and unsure which priorities will produce the best results, often just scaling the chaos.

CASE STUDY

I was recently coaching a therapist performing an initial consultation with a new patient. As a therapist, he diligently completed the subjective and objective examination, but he fell down the usual performance potholes. He gave a professional but overly technical explanation of his diagnosis and treatment plan.

What he didn't do was match the service benefits with patient wants. He didn't find out the consequences of inaction to the patient, he didn't address any assumptions or objections the patient may have had. Most strikingly – and I see this time and time again with therapists, regardless of how experienced they are – he failed to explore in a meaningful or emotional way how important it was for the patient to return to full health, ie the value of solving the problem.

In this instance, the patient was a gymnastics coach, but the therapist didn't probe deeply enough to identify why she was there. What was really at stake? Unfortunately, he didn't:

- Ask if she was a volunteer coach, or employed part-time or full-time

- Explore whether she was paid sick pay or would lose financial income through ill health

- Unearth how critical it was for her to avoid a period of rest and how it would affect her salary

- Notice how she became excited and hopeful when she talked about returning to gymnastics coaching as her students had an upcoming exam

- Unearth her buying motives

- Explain on an emotional level how he could help her return to gymnastics quickly

- Paint picture of her future self, uninjured, fully recovered, back to coaching

To be successful in a health business, your therapists need to have a holistic approach to the patient, putting the health issues into the context of the bigger picture: the patient's future self, aims and goals. It's crucial the therapist builds an emotional connection through empathy, understanding how the health issues affect the patient, identifying high-value problems worth solving and selling their solution in a way the patient can quickly understand because it resonates with their internal language.

In this case, we'll never know. The patient never came back, which was a lose-lose-lose for everyone involved: patient, therapist and business. As it occurred within a coaching environment, I console myself with the fact that it was an invaluable learning opportunity that will help prevent other patients from suffering a similar fate.

Cut the cost

When lost opportunities such as the one in the case study occur outside of a coaching environment, when they're happening in your health business day in and day out, it's really a failure. There are many opportunities for your therapists to develop deep and meaningful relationships with their patients in the treatment room, but all too often they go unnoticed every day. If your business connects with clear communication and unearths a mountain of value for both therapist and patient, it takes money off the table and builds a better future for all involved.

By now, I'm sure you realise that building valuable patient-therapist relationships with A-star self-funding patients until they achieve their aims and goals is a valid, fast-track, retention-based growth model. It represents a massive and mainly undiscovered opportunity for improving revenues, profit and growth which is lying dormant in most health businesses today.

I want to ask you:

- How much are wasted opportunities and low-value relationships costing you on a day-to-day, week-to-week basis in your health business?

- How much are mediocre sales skills costing your business in terms of lost patients, lost revenue and profits?

Let's find out what happens with an example of an altruistic therapist. Of their patients, 40% only come to two consultations, the remaining 60% attend five consultations on average. A top performer initiating a typical successful patient journey would see each patient for seven consultations on average at £50 per session. Both the altruistic therapist and the top performer see thirty new patients per month.

Average Consultations Attended	Revenue = Patients x Consultations x Cost £
40% of patients attend 2 consultations	30 patients x 40% = 12 patients x 2 consultations x £50 per consultation = **£1,200**
60% of patients attend 5 consultations	30 patients x 60% = 18 patients x 5 consultations x £50 per consultation = **£4,500**
Total revenue with altruistic therapist	£1,200 + £4,500 = **£5,700**
Successful patient journey is 7 consultations	30 patients x 7 consultations x £50 = **£10,500**
Lost revenue with altruistic therapist	£10,500 - £5,700 = **£4,800**

Lost revenue with altruistic therapist

By looking at this basic example, you can see that the altruistic therapist only billed £5,700, whereas a therapist trained in the Practice with Profit Way would have billed an extra £4,800. This represents an increase of approximately 84% on the revenue earned by the altruistic therapist. When we multiply this over a year, it's equivalent to £57,600 lost revenue per therapist.

Now let's look at how that impacts the lost revenues of a lifestyle health business with up to twelve therapists:

Number of FTE Therapists	Lost Revenue
1	£57,600
2	£115,200
3	£172,800
4	£230,400
5	£288,000
6	£345,600
7	£403,200
8	£460,800
9	£518,400
10	£576,000
11	£633,600
12	£691,200

Lost revenue costs

What can I say if that's not shocking enough for you? All that lost revenue is potentially lost profit for your business. If that's not enough to motivate you into stopping the rot and preventing your misguided altruistic therapists haemorrhaging revenue with each and every patient, nothing will.

When you're aware of and consider these lost opportunities across your whole team, per annum, you can see that leaving your therapists' interpersonal and sales skills undeveloped is a multiplier of lost revenue. I know you can do much better.

Future-proof your health business

If you are to survive and thrive as a health business for the long term, following the Practice with Profit Way and building valuable patient-therapist relationships with A-star self-funding patients until they achieve their aims and goals must be your number-one priority.

Healthcare is going through a major disruption with technology and artificial intelligence (AI) at the forefront. Arianna Huffington in her article 'The Annual Performance Review Is Dead' (2019) wrote about future workforce productivity, explaining that while AI will cost jobs, there are significant opportunities in sectors where humans are caring for other humans. These opportunities are centred on what cannot be automated: creativity, complex decision making, empathy, compassion, engagement and caring.

This is great news for the future of health businesses that want to gain an edge in the increasingly competitive market of helping people. I recommend you start future-proofing your health business right now, using the five-step Practice with Profit Way that I have detailed throughout this book. Empower your therapists with commercial skills in a caring culture, improve emotional engagement and retention, and build a high-performing, motivated and productive therapy team to cut the cost of running a health business and maximise revenues, profit and growth.

Cycle of care

The people in your health business are the most important assets you've got. Fundamentally, your role is to turn those assets into revenue and profit while minimising expense. You achieve this by investing in your people, which is especially rewarding when you consider the worsening recruitment landscape in the health industry.

The Practice with Profit Way teaches you how to build valuable patient-therapist relationships for growth and scale. This patient retention-based growth model achieves success with minimal costs by maximising the returns from the most valuable assets you have in your relationship business: your people.

To grow quickly with maximum profit, don't get distracted by the next marketing campaign, the next great breakthrough in treatment, the next new piece of equipment, machine or refurbishment. The quickest, easiest, most profitable way to achieve health business growth is to invest in your people: your therapists and patients. Rather than focusing on a traditional sales and marketing approach to grow your health business and leave your therapists to do their clinical best, solve your cycle of despair with the Practice with Profit cycle of care.

The cycle of care involves all three stakeholders investing in and taking better care of each other. It's critical you work through the process in the specific order shown in the diagram as you cannot expect your patients to become engaged with a longer lifetime value without them having being cared for first.

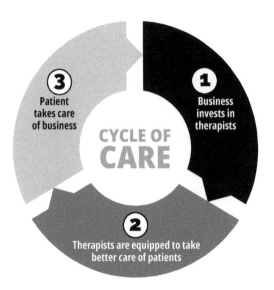

The process starts at the top with the health-business leadership team taking better care of their therapists by investing in their training. Equip your therapists with the tools and skills for success in a modern health business. I'm talking about the soft skills; the interpersonal skills; the clear communication, relationship and problem-solving skills. By equipping your team with these skills, you will grow their confidence and ability to achieve your health-business goals.

Your therapists will then be better equipped to take care of their patients, ie your customers. They will be able to identify and solve valuable problems, build emotional engagement, deliver improved patient outcomes and long-term relationships. They'll convert 100% of A-star self-funding patients into customers who commit to a successful course of treatment until they've achieved their aims and goals, maximising revenues and profit.

When this is happening to a high degree, then and only then will your patients take better care of your health business long term with improved loyalty and retention. You'll find that many will sign up for membership or subscription services.

As a team leader, if you follow the cycle of care, you'll have an engaged and productive clinical team taking great care of their current patients. With improved utilisation, revenue and profitability per employee, you'll be scaling your team and business for growth, minimising lost revenue and maximising profitability. Ensuring you're currently customer focused, you'll convert those customers into advocates for your health business as they recommend your services to family and friends. Your business will then become increasingly profitable, selling at premium prices and enjoying high margins by delivering extraordinary services to a large segment of ideal customers.

Layering the cycle of care

At Practice with Profit, we layer the cycle of care over the five-step Practice with Profit Way to build valuable patient-therapist relationships with A-star self-funding patients, leading them into a successful course of treatment until they achieve their aims and goals. It's a best-practice, highly leveraged, retention-based, cost-benefit approach to growth, as illustrated in this diagram.

Cost-benefit approach

- **Step 1: Culture.** In Step 1, focus on the first layer of the 80/20 principle, maximising your therapist utilisation and health-business capacity. This is achieved through maximising the number of FTE therapists in your business and the time they spend in one-to-one consultations, helping people.

- **Step 2: Connect.** In Step 2, you target the second layer of the 80/20 principle to maximise value. You accomplish this by building valuable patient-therapist relationships in the consultation room.

- **Step 3: Convert.** In Step 3, explore the third layer of the 80/20 principle and maximise conversion of A-star self-funding patients into customers who commit to a course of therapy as a fundamental starting point of their recovery journey. This razor-sharp focus on the ultimate aim of the initial consultation is critical to success, otherwise it's literally lose-lose-lose for everyone.

- **Step 4: Consult.** In Step 4, you go four layers deep into the 80/20 principle, to maximise value in each consultation. Using the tips and techniques I've shared, maximise the number of patient consultations by adding value, building engagement and retention, guiding your patients to recovery, achieving their unique aims and goals.

- **Step 5: Consistent.** In Step 5, you bring everything together under a best-practice management and leadership system to build a consistently high-performing therapy team for profit, growth and scale.

Benefits

There are many benefits to implementing this system to a high degree in your health business, but the top three are:

- **Health business mastery.** You'll build an aligned, productive, high-performing therapy team, each therapist having clinical mastery tailored to your health business. Your therapists will just 'get it'. Being unconsciously competent in interpersonal and stress-free sales, they'll consistently smash the financial growth targets of your company.

- **Retention membership business model.** You'll maximise patient engagement, retention and lifetime value, enjoying the stability of a recurring-revenue membership model. You'll maximise your ROI on your capital and people for growth and scale. Your business will switch from being new-patient focused to taking care of your current customers. The Practice with Profit Way is a long-term relationship model that drives revenue, profitability and growth.

- **Health business transformation.** When the Practice with Profit Way is working well, your patients will transform your health business. As a health-business leader, you'll no longer have to work in the business. You'll have confidence and freedom with a repeatable systemised process to multiply your profits and grow your practice with less stress and more freedom.

With the Practice with Profit Way aligned with the cycle of care, you'll escape the boom-and-bust cycle of despair where the bust months break you more than the boom months make you. Your business will stand out from the competition, selling at premium prices, enjoying high margins by delivering exceptional service to a large segment of ideal customers. The five-step Practice with Profit Way is a simple, proven solution which is central to achieving your desired business transformation.

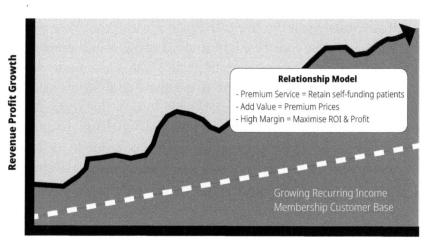

Relationship Model
- Premium Service = Retain self-funding patients
- Add Value = Premium Prices
- High Margin = Maximise ROI & Profit

Growing Recurring Income
Membership Customer Base

Revenue Profit Growth

Health Business Transformation

Profitable practice

Over my career, I've spent 30,000+ hours face-to-face with patients, coaching them on how to get better and achieve health and wellbeing transformations. At the same time, I've trained and coached my therapists how to have similar success. The unique methodology I've developed as a result deeply understands therapists' motivators and purpose. They want to help their patients achieve true health transformations, but their mindset, experience, knowledge and skills may be limiting them greatly.

I can see a better future because I know it doesn't have to be this way.

Through my extensive experience, I've become a sales expert, business leader and coach in the health and wellness industry. My unique vantage point, skillset and methodology will help your therapists achieve similar success and growth.

197

If you implement the five-step Practice with Profit Way to a high degree in your health business, I know your therapists will be able to convert all their patients into customers who commit to a successful course of treatment until they achieve their aims and goals. That's my big vision. It starts with one health business, with one therapist, with one patient. By extending outwards from the confines of a simple patient-therapist relationship, we can all as health-business leaders transform the health and wellbeing of a nation, one patient at a time.

Next steps

If you'd like to do a quick diagnostic to see how your health business currently measures up to the five steps of the Practice with Profit Way, assessing the quick wins you can implement into your health business today, please visit www.practicewithprofit.com/scorecard and fill in the online assessment tool. You'll get a bespoke report on the action steps you can implement into your health business straight away to multiply your profits and grow your practice with less stress and more freedom. If you have any questions, difficulties or struggles, I'm here to help. Just reach out via email or social media to share your ups and downs with me.

I wish you all the success in implementing the Practice with Profit Way and transforming your health business for profit, growth and scale. Good luck.

Paul Baker

www.practicewithprofit.com
paul@practicewithprofit.com

References

Chapter One – The Practice With Profit Way

Koch, R (2007) *The 80/20 Principle: The secret of achieving more with less*. 2nd ed. London: Clays

Marshall, P (2013) *80/20 Sales And Marketing: The definitive guide to working less and making more*. USA: Entrepreneur Press

Guest, R (2017) *Built To Grow: How to deliver accelerated, sustained and profitable business growth*. Padstow: Wiley

Chapter Two – Step 1: Culture

Miller, D (2017) *Building A Story Brand: Clarify your message so customers will listen*. Nashville: HarperCollins Leadership

Collins, J (2001) *Good to Great: Why some companies make the leap – and others don't*. US: Collins Business

Steeper, C and Stockdale, S (2016) *Motivating People In A Week*. 2nd ed. London: John Murray Learning

Pink, D (2011) *Drive: The surprising truth about what motivates us.* Edinburgh: Canongate Books

Peters, S (2012) *The Chimp Paradox: The acclaimed mind management programme to help you achieve success, confidence and happiness.* London: Vermillion

Chapter Three – Step 2: Connect

Zieg, J (ed) (1980) *A Teaching Seminar with Milton H. Erickson.* New York: Brunner-Mazel

Maitland, G (1964) *Vertebral Manipulation.* 5th ed. Oxford: Butterworth-Heinemann

Blount, J (2010) *People Buy You: The real secret to what matters most in business.* New Jersey: Wiley & Sons

Priestley, D (2017) *24 Assets: Create a digital, scalable, valuable and fun business that will thrive in a fast changing world.* London: Rethink Press

Pink, D (2018) *To Sell Is Human: The surprising truth about persuading, convincing, and influencing others.* 2nd ed. London: Canongate Books

Chapter Five – Step 4: Consult

Warrillow, J (2015) *The Automatic Customer: Creating a subscription business in any industry.* London: Portfolio Penguin

Chapter Six – Step 5: Consistent

Priestley, D (2017) *24 Assets: Create a digital, scalable, valuable and fun business that will thrive in a fast changing world.* Great Britain: Rethink Press

'What Is Net Promoter?' (2017) [online] Available at: www.netpromoter.com/know [Accessed 17 April 2019]

Conclusion

Jones, M and Rivett, D (2003) *Clinical Reasoning for Manual Therapists.* Edinburgh: Elsevier

Chopra, D and Kafatos, M (2017) *You Are the Universe: Discovering Your Cosmic Self and Why It Matters.* London: Penguin Random House

Lee, D (2010) *The Pelvic Girdle: An integration of clinical expertise and research.* Edinburgh: Elsevier

Huffington, A (2019) 'The Annual Performance Review Is Dead'. Productivity [online], 23 January 2019. Available at: https://thriveglobal.in/stories/the-annual-performance-review-is-dead

Acknowledgements

For years, I've been thinking of writing a book sharing insights from inside the consulting room, insights on the importance of interpersonal and sales skills in building valuable long-term relationships with self-funding patients, as a valid retention-based model to health business growth. Thank you to those who listened to me, giving me the time, energy and wisdom to help me transform my ideas and insights into a book.

Thank you to the many tens of thousands of patients who've trusted me and my team with their injuries, thoughts, hopes and dreams to guide them to recovery. Without them I couldn't do what I do and could not have learned what I've learned.

Thanks must go to the goPhysio team. The content for this book has been honed and sharpened during the many team training sessions we've had over the years. I'm sure you've politely endured as I've simplified my message into the five-step Practice with Profit Way. Thank you for your flexible mindset and willingness to challenge the status quo to deliver our profitable practice.

Thank you to Niall, my business mentor, who has helped us implement much of the Practice with Profit methods into our practice. Your extensive experience and guidance has been greatly appreciated.

Thank you to Steve, a business mentor and friend, for teaching me about the intricacies of team engagement, motivation and coaching principles, and for continuing to help us at goPhysio to build our motivated and high-performing therapy team.

A big thank you to Daniel Priestley for his business courses, guidance and introduction to Lucy McCarraher at Rethink Press, who developed the W.R.I.T.E.R. Process specifically for experienced professionals to share their expertise with the world, in book format. Without her books, guidance, webinars and emails, this book wouldn't have ever materialised.

Thank you to Kathleen and Alison, my editors at Rethink, who made the editing and publishing process simple and straightforward. Your experience and expertise has helped me deliver a book that is easy to read. Your guidance is much appreciated.

A big thank you also to my beta readers:

Amanda, a fellow health-business owner and long-term friend. Our energetic phone calls discussing the cut and thrust of health business ownership continue to be entertaining and fun.

Kim, our clinical lead, who is well versed in the Practice with Profit Way. You offered great attention to detail and insight into the content, keeping me focused and on track in your kind and caring way.

Alan, our occupational profiling expert, who has helped build the great team we have today. Thank you for always offering me clear, direct, invaluable advice, and for helping me avoid expensive and timely mistakes.

You all persisted during your own downtime through early, difficult-to-read manuscripts, and I'll always be grateful.

Thank you to Warren, my illustrator, who spent a lot of time understanding my ideas, working through iterations and bringing them to life in his designs and graphic illustrations.

Thank you to Fiona, my wife, life and business partner. I know it hasn't been easy, but hopefully it has been a bit of fun. Our often-heated discussions have helped me channel my experience into a book that will help others achieve similar success.

Thank you to my children, Maxwell, Finnian and Annabelle, for the space and understanding you've given me, with my absenteeism at breakfast and some weekends. Without that time, this book wouldn't have been completed.

Finally, thanks to my dad, mum and family. I grew up amidst a family business, with some long hours, late nights and plenty of craic. I enjoyed the rewards, and it taught me the value of following my interests and passions.

The Author

In 2001, at age twenty-six, Paul opened his first health business, goPhysio Ltd. He has since spent over 30,000 hours in face-to-face consultations, guiding and coaching patients to recovery. His passion is combining clinical mastery with commercial acumen, building profitable practices around valuable relationships with self-funding patients, and guiding them to long-term health transformations.

He has spent thousands of hours coaching and mentoring his team to improve their interpersonal (relationship and communication), sales and commercial skills to repeat his successes inside the consultation room.

Since he developed his methodology into the Practice with Profit Way, he and his team have built goPhysio into a profitable practice that employs 13 full-time team members. Self-funding patients make up 97% of the customer base and over 200 are in recurring revenue membership services.

Following this success, Paul has founded the Practice with Profit online health business accelerator programme. Its purpose is to equip like-minded health-business leaders and therapists with the training and tools to transform their businesses – multiplying their profits and growing their practices with minimum stress and maximum freedom.

Paul has a postgraduate diploma in independent practice and is the host of *The Sales Therapist* podcast on iTunes.

You can learn more and contact Paul at:

🌐 www.practicewithprofit.com

✉ paul@practicewithprofit.com

in www.linkedin.com/in/paultbaker

f www.facebook.com/practicewithprofit

🐦 @PracticeWProfit

📷 @PracticewithProfit

Lightning Source UK Ltd.
Milton Keynes UK
UKHW040951291019
352508UK00005B/206/P